GETTING STARTED WITH PEACHTREE COMPLETE ACCOUNTING 2005

GETTING STARTED WITH PEACHTREE COMPLETE ACCOUNTING 2005

Elaine Heldstab
METROPOLITAN COMMUNITY COLLEGES
Kansas City, Missouri

VP/Editorial Director: Jeff Shelstad
Acquisitions Editor: Wendy Craven
Senior Project Managr: Kerri Tomasso
Associate Director, Manufacturing: Vincent Scelta
Production Editor & Buyer: Carol O'Rourke
Printer/Binder: Bind-Rite Graphics

Pearson Prentice Hall™ is a trademark of Pearson Education, Inc.

10 9 8 7 6 5 4
ISBN 0-13-219681-6

Dedicated to my very understanding mother, Madeline.

TABLE OF CONTENTS

PREFACE

Welcome Students and Instructors!

Getting Started with Peachtree Complete Accounting 2005 was written to provide the accounting student with an overview of how the manual concepts taught in the introductory accounting classes can be applied within a computerized accounting environment. While the book is written using instructions for Peachtree Complete Accounting 2005, the concepts learned can be applied to learning many of the other computerized accounting programs available to businesses.

The book also contains a quick, refresher course in Windows but does not attempt to teach those skills in a comprehensive manner. It is presumed that the user has at a minimum, the basic accounting skills taught in the first accounting course. The activities will require the use of the company data files available on the instructor CD-ROM as well as on the Educational version of Peachtree Complete Accounting 2005 which is available from Prentice Hall. This option allows the student to take home a full, working copy of the program as well as the data files.

The book contains 10 chapters of computer workshops, 5 of which contain mini-practice sets to allow the student to practice the concepts being taught in that chapter as well as the chapters prior to the practice set. For students: All of the data files that accompany this text can be downloaded from www.prenhall.com/compaccounting. For instructors: Downloadable Excel Solutions to the problems can be found by going to www.prenhall.com/compaccounting. You will need the access codes provided by your Prentice Hall Sales Representative.

Suggested Sequence

The following chart summaries the computerized accounting materials contained in the text and suggests the order in which they could best be assigned.

Assignment

1.   Part A of the Computerized Accounting Appendix

2.   Part B of the Computerized Accounting Appendix

3.   Part C of the Computerized Accounting Appendix

4.   Computer Workshop (Chapter 1)

5.   Computer Workshop (Chapter 2) The Atlas Company

7.   Computer Workshop (Chapter 3) The Zell Company

8.   Computer Workshop (Chapter 4) Valdez Realty Mini Practice Set

9.   Computer Workshop (Chapter 5) Pete's Market Mini Practice Set

10.   Computer Workshop (Chapter 6) Part A The Mars Company

14.   Computer Workshop (Chapter 6) Part B Abby's Toy House Mini Practice Set

15.   Computer Workshop (Chapter 7) The Corner Dress Shop Mini Practice Set

16.   Computer Workshop (Chapter 8) The Paint Place Mini Practice Set

17.   Computer Workshop (Chapter 9) Bellwether Garden Supply

18.   Computer Workshop (Chapter 10) Lindquist Custom Woodworking

CHAPTER 1

System Requirements, Installation, Settings, Backing up and Restoring data files

Before starting on this assignment, read and complete the tasks discussed in Part A of the appendix at the back of this book.

SYSTEM REQUIREMENTS

The recommended minimum software and hardware requirements your computer system needs to run both Windows and Peachtree Complete Accounting 2005 successfully are:

- IBM Compatible 300 MHz Pentium II computer minimum; IBM Compatible 450 MHz Pentium II or higher recommended

- Windows XP (Service Pack 1)/2000 (Service Pack 3)/ME/98 SE/NT 4.0 (Service Pack 6a). Product will not operate in a Windows Terminal Server Environment using Windows Terminal Services.

- 64 MB RAM minimum; 128 MB RAM recommended

- 110MB-250 MB free hard disk space

- Internet Explorer 6.0 required. Microsoft Internet Explorer 6.0 is included on the Peachtree CD. Requires 70MB (or higher) for installation.

- Display settings of at least High Color (16bit). SVGA video. 800 x 600 resolution with small fonts.

- Printers supported by Windows XP/2000/ME/98/NT 4.0

- Online features require Internet access. Minimum connection speed depends on service.

- In-product demos require Macromedia® Flash™ Player.

- Mouse or compatible pointing device

- CD-ROM drive

- To install the audio tutorial and online documentation, an additional 60-70 MB free hard disk space is required.

- To use Microsoft Office Excel, Excel 2000, Excel 2005, or Excel 2003 is required

- To use Microsoft Office Word, Word 2000, Word 2005, or Word 2003 is required

- Multi-User optimized for Windows XP/2000/98/NT 4.0 (peer-to-peer network), Windows 2000 Server, Windows Server 2003, Windows Small Business Server 2003, Windows NT 4.0 server, or Novell NetWare Network 5.1, 6.0, or 6.5. Recommended for 5 users or less.

Installing Peachtree Complete Accounting 2005/Student Data Files

CD-ROM CONTENTS

The Peachtree Complete Accounting 2005 installation and program files (in condensed form) and the Student Data Files for use in completing the Computer Workshops are on the CD-ROM that accompanies this text.

Installing Peachtree Complete 2005 Software

To install Peachtree Complete Accounting 2005 on your hard disk (c: drive)

1. Start Windows
2. Make sure that no other programs are running on your system.
3. Insert the CD from the back of your text book in your CD-ROM drive.
4. The opening window for Peachtree should be displayed

    Note: If windows does not automatically display you will need to Click on the Start button; then click on Run.

    Type d:\autorun.exe and press the ENTER key. For d, substitute the letter of your CD-ROM drive.

5. Click on the Peachtree Accounting title.

6. Accept the license agreement.

7. Select the standard setup.

8. Select Yes to install an icon on your desktop.

9. The program installs in the folder C:\Program Files\Peachtree\peachw

Installation Default Settings

In the 2005 version of Peachtree Complete Accounting, you may encounter some differences in your screens to the screen captures contained in this book. This is due in part to the fact that Peachtree will install to one set of settings on a machine that has contained a previous version of Peachtree and to a second set of setting on a machine to which you are installing Peachtree for the first time. In order to ensure that your screens will be the same as those in this book, make or confirm the following selections from the Options menu item.

1. Open the Peachtree software.

2. Click close on the open existing file screen

3. Select **Global** from the **Options** menu

4. Select the Accounting tab.

5. In the section entitled Hide General Ledger Accounts, remove any checkmarks from the three boxes in that section by left clicking on the checkmark.

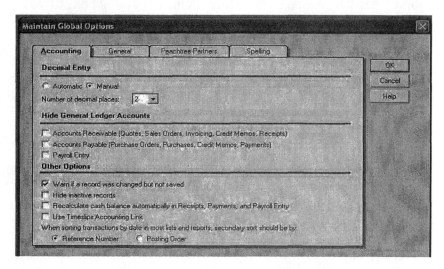

6. Click OK and exit Peachtree to make the changes permanent.

Installing Student Data Files

1. After the Peachtree complete software is loaded you will need to install the company data files provided on the CD that came with this book.

2. Click on Company Files located on the CD and extract the files (they are zip files) to the following folder C:\Program Files\Peachtree\Company.

Using Peachtree Complete Accounting 2005 on a Network

Peachtree Complete Accounting 2005 can be used in a network environment as long as each student uses a separate Student Data Files source to store his or her data files. Students should consult with their instructor and/or network administrator for specific procedures regarding program installation and any special printing procedures required for proper network operation.

Peachtree will run most efficiently if the student data files are installed on a hard drive. This can occur on the local hard drive or in a unique student folder on a network drive. Since it is possible that student files may be tampered with between class sessions, it is recommended that students back up and restore their files with a floppy disk (or jump drive) each class day. Peachtree's back up and restore functions are quick and easy to follow.

Opening a File in Peachtree Complete

As with any other Windows program, files in Peachtree are opened by using the **Open Company** option from the **File** menu. Double click on the Peachtree icon on your desktop. Select **Open Company** option from the **File** menu. Peachtree will then open up an Open Company dialog box where you can tell Peachtree where to find the files you need. The files that have been supplied with this text for the sample companies should reside in the same directory as the Peachtree program files, generally "Peachw\Company". Each company will have its own folder that can be read by the Open Company dialog box. If you do not see these files when you first open the box, you may need to change the directory or drive to one your instructor will specify. The directory should contain the company data files shown below.

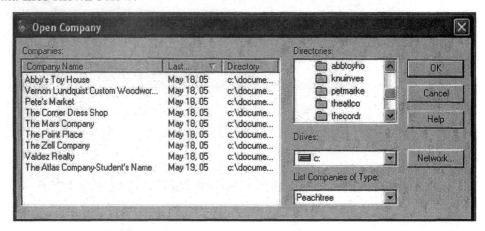

Backing up a File in Peachtree Complete

Before starting any assignment, it is suggested that you create a backup of the company data file in the event you need to restore back to the beginning of the assignment.

Peachtree has the capability to quickly and easily back up your data to protect against accidental loss.

1. Let's say we wish to backup **Stone Arbor Landscaping** (this is one of the sample companies that comes with the software). We would open that company using the **Open Company** feature from the **File** menu option.

2. We would then select **Back Up** from the **File** menu option. This will bring up the Back Up Company dialogue box as follows:

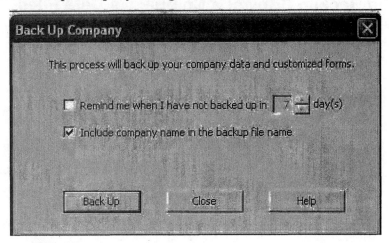

3. Click in the box next to **Include company name in the backup file name**. This will make Peachtree use Stone Arbor Landscaping in the filename it selects for the backup. You could also use this dialogue box to have Peachtree provide a reminder at periodic intervals but we will leave this option alone for now. Press **Back Up Now** to continue.

4. You are now presented with a Save Back Up for the Stone Arbor Landscaping dialog box as follows:

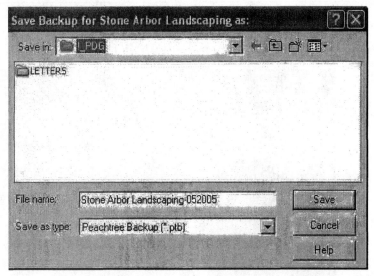

5. Peachtree will save your data files into one compressed .ptb file to any drive or path you specify including a floppy drive. It defaults to the location where the program files are stored and specifically to the folder where the company files are kept which is the !_PDG directory. Use the **Save in** lookup box to save the files to a location specified by your instructor. This could be a network drive, a student floppy disk or even the local hard drive. Click **Save** and then **Ok** to complete the process. You now have a back up of your data. You should consider saving each and every day to protect yourself against possible loss. Peachtree will use the

date as part of the backup's name so you could have a separate backup for each day. You do not have to accept the name Peachtree assigns and you can use a name with more meaning to you. You should be able to fit about 4 different backups on a floppy disk.

Using the Backup Copy of a Company's Data Files

At certain times in the assignments you are asked to make a backup copy of a company's data files. There are several reasons why you might wish to access the backup copy of a company's data files. For example, you may not have printed a required report in an assignment before advancing the period to a new month or before adding additional transactions. You may have several errors and simply want to start an assignment over or to a point prior to the errors rather than correct the mistakes.

If you backup your data using a different filename each day, you will have the option of restoring from any of these files. It would be wise to indicate in your text the point at which you created each backup so you will know what transactions have been completed at each of the backup's dates.

How to Repeat or Restart an Assignment

You always have the option to repeat an assignment for additional practice or start over on an assignment. You simply restore the sample company files back to their original state using the Backup created at the start of the assignment. The procedure for restoring a file is very similar:

1. Open the company whose files you wish to restore. Let's say we wish to restore the Stone Arbor Landscaping backup. We would open that company using the **Open** feature from the **File** menu option.

2. While in the Menu Window, select **Restore** from the **File** menu option. This will bring up the Restore Wizard dialogue boxes as follows:

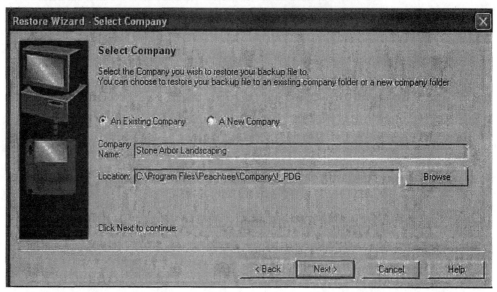

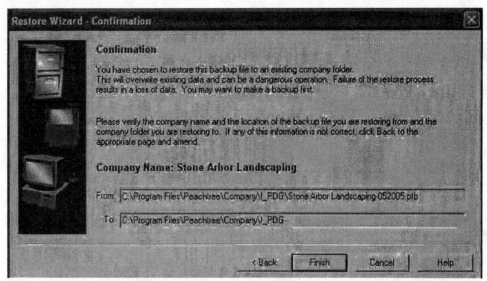

3. Peachtree will default to the folder where the regular company files are kept. If you are keeping your backups on a floppy or on a drive/path other than the one Peachtree is defaulting to, you must use the **Browse** option to change the drive and select the correct path from the options given. You may have several backups made at different points in time so be sure to select the correct one. In the example above, there is only one backup so we would select Stone Arbor Landscaping-052005. After you have selected the correct filename, click on **Finish.**

CHAPTER 2

Journalizing, Posting, General Ledger, Trial Balance, and Chart of Accounts

How to Open the Company Data Files

1. Click on the Start button. Point to Programs; point to the Peachtree folder and select Peachtree Complete Accounting 2005. Your desktop may have the Peachtree icon allowing for a quicker entrance into the program by double clicking it.

2. Go to the **File** menu and select **Open company** select the **The Atlas Company**. You may be initially presented with the Peachtree Today window. If so, simply close it. Your screen should then look something like the illustration below:

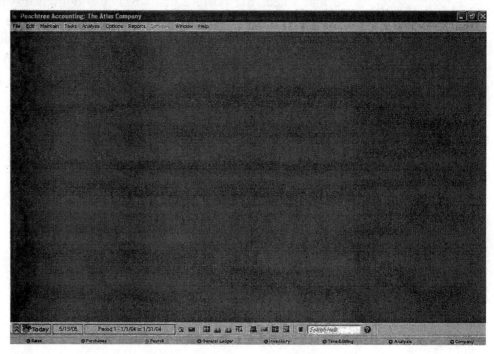

If you are missing the navigation aids at the bottom of the screen, you can activate them under the **Options** menu. Select **View Navigation Aid**. It will remain on until you turn it off. This feature offers an alternative way to access the different features of Peachtree.

3. Click on the **Maintain** menu option. Then select **Company Information**. The program will respond by bringing up a dialogue box allowing the user to edit/add information about the company.

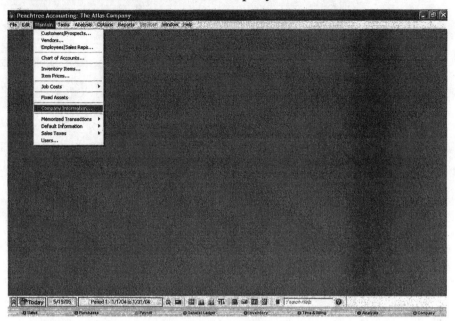

4. It is important for you to be able to identify the specific reports that you print for each assignment as your own, particularly if you are using a computer that shares a printer with other computers. Peachtree Complete Accounting 2005 prints the name of the company you are working with at the top of each report. To personalize your reports so that you can identify both the company and your printed reports, the company name needs to be modified to include your name:

    a. Click in the **Company Name** entry field at the end of **The Atlas Company**. If it is already highlighted, press the right arrow key.

    b. Add a dash and your name **"-Student Name"** or initials to the end of the company name. Your screen will look similar to the one shown below:

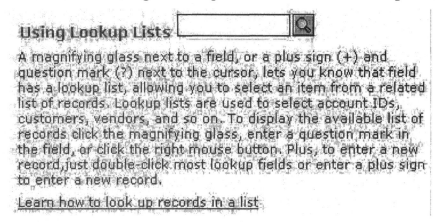

Maintain Company Information

Company Name: The Atlas Company-Student's Name

Address:

City, ST Zip:

Country:

Telephone: Web Site:

Fax: E-mail:

State Employer ID: Fed Employer ID:

State Unemployment ID: Form of Business: Sole Proprietorship

Directory: C:\Documents and Settings\Owner\My Documents\Prentice Hall Received Fil

Posting Method: ▶ Real-time   Accounting Method: Accrual

Direct Deposit: ▶ Inactive   ☐ Use Audit Trail

Peachtree Payroll Service: ▶ Inactive

c. Click on the **OK** button to return to the Menu Window.

How to Record a General Journal Entry

5. The owner of The Atlas Company has invested $10,000 in the business. Select **General Journal Entry** from the **Tasks** menu to open the General Journal dialog box. Enter the date 1/1/04 into the **Date** field (the date the transaction occurred); press the TAB key; enter **"MEMO"** into the **Reference** field (reference number or notation you wish to associate with a general journal entry and/or the source document that authorizes the entry) and press **TAB**.

    Note that pressing **ENTER** will also move you from field to field.

6. With the flashing insertion point positioned in the **Account No** field, click on the lookup button (magnifying glass icon) and double click on "1110 Cash". The program will enter the account number into the **Account No** field and the flashing insertion point will move to the **Description** field.

Using Lookup Lists [🔍]

A magnifying glass next to a field, or a plus sign (+) and question mark (?) next to the cursor, lets you know that field has a lookup list, allowing you to select an item from a related list of records. Lookup lists are used to select account IDs, customers, vendors, and so on. To display the available list of records click the magnifying glass, enter a question mark in the field, or click the right mouse button. Plus, to enter a new record, just double-click most lookup fields or enter a plus sign to enter a new record.

Learn how to look up records in a list

7. Enter "Initial investment of cash by owner" into the **Description** field and press TAB to move to the **Debit** field.

8. Enter "10000" into the **Debit** field. Press the TAB key three times to move through the **Credit** and **Job** fields.

9. With the flashing insertion point again positioned in the **Account No** field, click on the lookup button. Double click on "3110 Owner's Capital". Use the scroll bar if the account is not visible in the lookup list. Press TAB to move to the **Description** field. This should repeat the description information entered in the debit entry.

10. Press the TAB key twice to move to the **Credit** field. Enter "10000." Hit TAB twice to move the cursor back to the **Account No** field. This completes the data you need to enter into the General Journal dialog box to record the journal entry for the initial investment of cash by the owner. Your screen should look something like this:

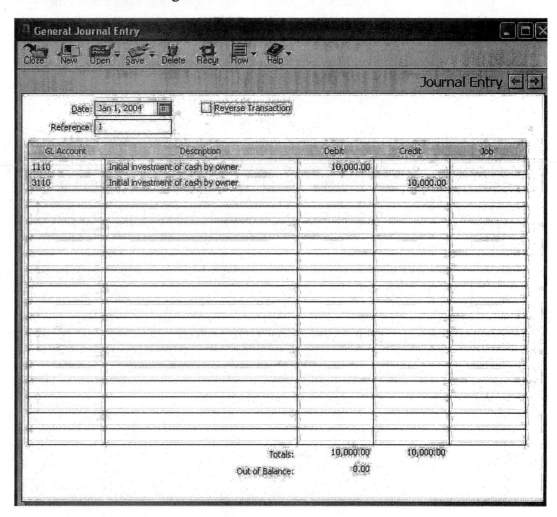

Review the Journal Entry Before Posting

11. Before posting this transaction, you should verify that the transaction data are correct by reviewing the journal entry.

12. If you have made an error, use the following editing techniques to correct the error(s).

How to Edit an Entry Prior to Posting

Editing a General Journal Entry

♦ Using your mouse, click in the field that contains the error. This will highlight the selected text box information so that you can change it.

- ◆ Type the correct information; then press the TAB key to enter it. You may then either TAB to other fields needing corrections or again use the mouse to click in the proper field.

- ◆ If you have selected an incorrect account, use the pull down menu to select the correct account. This will replace the incorrect account with the correct account.

- ◆ Note that even though the **Save** icon will be available if the entry is out of balance, Peachtree will not allow you to post until the entry is in balance.

- ◆ To discard an entry and start over, click on the **Delete** icon. You will not be given the opportunity to verify this step so be sure you want to delete the transaction before selecting this option.

- ◆ Review the journal entry for accuracy after any editing corrections.

How to Post an Entry

13. After verifying that the journal entry is correct, click on the **Save** icon to post this transaction. A blank General Journal dialog box is displayed, ready for additional General Journal transactions to be recorded. Peachtree has added a 1 to our memo in the **Reference** field and will do so as long as we remain in this input box. To keep the same reference for multiple entries on the same day, do not post between transactions.

Record Additional Transactions

14. Record the following additional journal entries. Enter the **Date** listed for each transaction (you may use the "+" key to advance the date or use the calendar icon next to the field to select the date from a calendar). Enter "MEMO" into the **Reference** text box for each transaction or accept Peachtree's additional number added to MEMO by pressing TAB:

2004
Jan.
- 1   Paid rent for two months in advance, $400.
- 3   Purchased office supplies on account, $100.
- 9   Billed a customer for fees earned, $1,500.
- 13   Paid telephone bill, $180.
- 20   Owner withdrew $500 from the business.
- 27   Received $450 for fees earned.
- 31   Paid salaries expense, $700.

15. After you have posted the additional journal entries, click on the close button to close the General Journal dialog box. This will restore the menu window.

16. To move between the journal entries use the arrow buttons on the journal entry screen

Journal Entry ← →

How to Display and Print a General Journal

17. Select **General Ledger** from the **Reports** menu to bring up reports associated with the general ledger such as the **General Journal** and the **Trial Balance**. Select **General Journal** from the report selection window to bring up the report. You may also use the General Ledger navigation folder at the bottom of your screen to provide you with General Ledger options including reports. Single click on the **General Ledger** folder at the bottom

of your screen and then single click **General Journal**. You will be taken to an options screen for the report. Accept all defaults by clicking on the **OK** button. Your screen should display something similar to this:

The Atlas Company-Student's Name					
General Journal					
For the Period From Jan 1, 2004 to Jan 31, 2004					
Filter Criteria includes: Report order is by Date. Report is printed with Accounts having Zero Amounts and with Truncated Transaction Descriptions and in Detail Format.					
Date	Account ID	Reference	Trans Description	Debit Amt	Credit Amt
1/1/04	1110	Memo	Initial investment of cash by owner	10,000.00	
	3110		Initial investment of cash by owner		10,000.00
1/1/04	1140	Memo1	Prepaid rent	400.00	
	1110		Prepaid rent		400.00
1/3/04	1150	Memo2	Purchased office supplies on account	100.00	
	2110		Purchased office supplies on account		100.00
1/9/04	1120	Memo3	Performed services on account	1,500.00	
	4110		Performed services on account		1,500.00
1/13/04	5150	Memo4	Paid telephone bill	180.00	
	1110		Paid telephone bill		180.00
1/20/04	3120	Memo5	Owner withdrawal	500.00	
	1110		Owner withdrawal		500.00
1/27/04	1110	Memo6	Performed services for cash	450.00	
	4110		Performed services for cash		450.00
1/31/04	5120	Memo7	Paid salaries expense	700.00	
	1110		Paid salaries expense		700.00
		Total		13,830.00	13,830.00

18. The scroll bars can be used to advance the display to view other portions of the report. Note: You may display the entire General Journal Display window by clicking the maximize icon.

19. Click on the **Print** icon to print the General Journal. If you experience any difficulties with your printer (for example, the type size is too small), refer to Part C of the appendix of this text book for information on how to adjust the print and display settings.

What to Do if You Posted an Incorrect Entry

20. Review your printed General Journal. If you note an error at this point, it can be easily fixed. With the General Journal report on your screen, place your cursor over the incorrect entry (it will resemble a magnifying glass with a "z" in the center). Double click on the entry you wish to correct and you will be taken to the **General Journal Entry** window that contains the entry. You may edit a posted transaction using the same procedures as editing an unposted transaction. After making the necessary changes, click on the **Save** icon to save your changes. You will be returned to your report where you can view the changes made.

How to Display and Print a General Ledger Report

21. Click on the **Close** icon to close the General Journal report. If you originally used the menu method to bring up the General Journal report, you are taken back to the report selection window where you can select **General Ledger**. If you originally used the navigation aid folder to bring up the report, you must again select the **General Ledger** folder and select **General Ledger** from the report options given to you. Your screen will look something like this:

The Atlas Company-Student's Name
General Ledger
For the Period From Jan 1, 2004 to Jan 31, 2004
Filter Criteria includes: Report order is by ID. Report is printed with Truncated Transaction Descriptions and in Detail Format.

Account ID Account Description	Date	Reference	Jrnl	Trans Description	Debit Amt	Credit Amt	Balance
1110 Cash	1/1/04			Beginning Balance			
	1/1/04	Memo	GENJ	Initial investment of c	10,000.00		
	1/1/04	Memo1	GENJ	Prepaid rent		400.00	
	1/13/04	Memo4	GENJ	Paid telephone bill		180.00	
	1/20/04	Memo5	GENJ	Owner withdrawal		500.00	
	1/27/04	Memo6	GENJ	Performed services for	450.00		
	1/31/04	Memo7	GENJ	Paid salaries expense		700.00	
				Current Period Change	10,450.00	1,780.00	8,670.00
	1/31/04			Ending Balance			8,670.00
1120 Accounts Receivable	1/1/04			Beginning Balance			
	1/9/04	Memo3	GENJ	Performed services on	1,500.00		
				Current Period Change	1,500.00		1,500.00
	1/31/04			Ending Balance			1,500.00
1140 Prepaid Rent	1/1/04			Beginning Balance			
	1/1/04	Memo1	GENJ	Prepaid rent	400.00		
				Current Period Change	400.00		400.00
	1/31/04			Ending Balance			400.00
1150 Office Supplies	1/1/04			Beginning Balance			
	1/3/04	Memo2	GENJ	Purchased office suppli	100.00		
				Current Period Change	100.00		100.00
	1/31/04			Ending Balance			100.00
2110 Accounts Payable	1/1/04			Beginning Balance			
	1/3/04	Memo2	GENJ	Purchased office suppli		100.00	

23. You will not see the entire report on the screen (or in the capture above). The scroll bars can be used to advance the display to view other portions of the report. You may also double click your mouse on any transaction to bring up the entry window for that transaction.

24. Click on the **Print** icon to print the General Ledger report.

How to Display and Print a Trial Balance

25. Click on the close button to close the General Ledger report and return to the reports selection window. Click on the General Ledger Trial Balance option. Your screen will look something like this:

The Atlas Company-Student's Name
General Ledger Trial Balance
As of Jan 31, 2004
Filter Criteria includes: Report order is by ID. Report is printed in Detail Format.

Account ID	Account Description	Debit Amt	Credit Amt
1110	Cash	8,670.00	
1120	Accounts Receivable	1,500.00	
1140	Prepaid Rent	400.00	
1150	Office Supplies	100.00	
2110	Accounts Payable		100.00
3110	Owner's Capital		10,000.00
3120	Owner's Withdrawals	500.00	
4110	Fees Earned		1,950.00
5120	Salaries Expense	700.00	
5150	Telephone Expense	180.00	
	Total	12,050.00	12,050.00

26. The scroll bar can be used to advance the display to view other portions of the report. You may also display zero balance accounts by clicking on the **Options** icon and clicking the box next to **Include Accounts with Zero Amounts**. Clicking on **OK** will return you to the report.

27. Click on the **Print** icon to print the Trial Balance with or without zero balances.

How to Display and Print a Chart of Accounts

28. Again click on the close button to close the Trial Balance report. Select **Chart of Accounts** from the report selection window. Your screen will look something like this:

Account ID	Account Description	Active?	Account Type
1110	Cash	Yes	Cash
1120	Accounts Receivable	Yes	Accounts Receivable
1140	Prepaid Rent	Yes	Other Current Assets
1150	Office Supplies	Yes	Other Current Assets
1210	Office Equipment	Yes	Fixed Assets
1221	Accum. Depr- Office Equipment	Yes	Accumulated Depreciation
1230	Automobile	Yes	Fixed Assets
1241	Accum. Depr- Automobile	Yes	Accumulated Depreciation
1250	Store Equipment	Yes	Fixed Assets
1261	Accum Depr- Store Equipment	Yes	Accumulated Depreciation
2110	Accounts Payable	Yes	Accounts Payable
3110	Owner's Capital	Yes	Equity-doesn't close
3120	Owner's Withdrawals	Yes	Equity-gets closed
3130	Retained Earnings	Yes	Equity-Retained Earnings
4110	Fees Earned	Yes	Income
5110	Rent Expense	Yes	Expenses
5120	Salaries Expense	Yes	Expenses
5150	Telephone Expense	Yes	Expenses

The Atlas Company-Student's Name
Chart of Accounts
As of Jan 31, 2004
Filter Criteria includes: Report order is by ID. Report is printed with Accounts having Zero Amounts and in Detail Format.

29. Click on the close button to close the Chart of Accounts window and return to the Menu Window.

How to Save your Work During a Current Work Session

30. There is no need to save your work in Peachtree. Each time you make a change and click save, your work is automatically saved. However, You should back up your work after each session following the instructions in Chapter 1.

How to Exit from the Program

31. Click on the Menu Window **File** menu; then click on Exit to end the current work session and return to your Windows desktop. Your work will automatically be saved unlike many other Windows based programs which require you to save before exiting.

32. You can exit from Peachtree Complete Accounting 2005 at any time during a current work session from any window that offers the **File** menu. You may be asked if you wish to save any unposted work. It is recommended that you always say yes.

CHAPTER 3

Compound Journal Entries, Adjusting Entries, and Printing Financial Reports

How to Open the Company Data Files

1. Double click on Peachtree Complete 2005 icon on your desktop to open the software program. If you do not have an icon you can go to Start, select Programs and select Peachtree Complete Accounting 2005.

2. Click on **File** and select **Open Company** select the **The Zell Company**.

   You should back up your work before starting each chapter following instructions in Chapter 1.

How to Add Your Name to the Company Name

3. Click on the **Maintain** menu option. Then select **Company Information**. The program will respond by bringing up a dialogue box allowing the user to edit/add information about the company.

4. Click in the **Company Name** entry field at the end of **The Zell Company**. If it is already highlighted, press the right arrow key. Add a dash and your name "**-Student Name**" or initials to the end of the company name. You may use initials only if practical. Click on the OK button to return to the Menu Window.

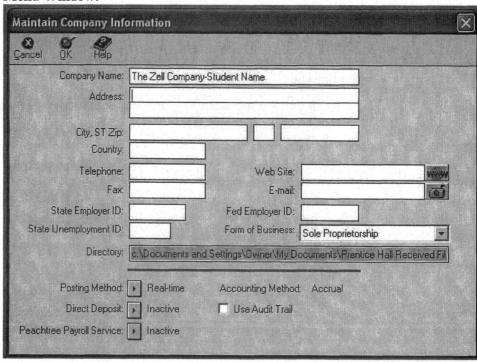

How to Record a Compound Journal Entry

5. Compound journal entries can also be recorded in the General Journal dialog box. The owner of The Zell Company has made an investment in the business consisting of $5,000 in cash and an automobile valued at $12,000. Select **General Journal Entry** from the **Tasks** menu to open the General

Journal dialog box. Enter the date 1/1/04 into the **Date** field; press the TAB key; enter "MEMO" into the **Reference** field and press TAB.

6. With the flashing insertion point positioned in the **Account No** field, click on the lookup button (magnifying glass icon) and double click on "1110 Cash". The program will enter the account number into the **Account No** field and the flashing insertion point will move to the **Description** field. Enter "Initial investment by owner" into this field and press TAB to move to the **Debit** field. Enter "5000" and press TAB three times to move back to the **Account No** field.

7. With the flashing insertion point positioned in the **Account No** field, click on the lookup button (magnifying glass icon) and double click on "1230 Automobile". Press TAB to move to the **Description** field. This should repeat the description from the first line by default. Press the TAB key again to move to the **Debit** field. Enter "12000". Hit TAB three times to move the cursor back to the **Account No** field. You should now have two debit entries.

8. With the flashing insertion point positioned in the **Account No** field, click on the pull down menu and double click on "3110 Owner's Capital". Press TAB to move to the **Description** field. This should repeat the information entered in step 6 by default. Press the TAB key again twice to move to the **Credit** field. Enter 17000. Hit TAB twice to move the cursor back to the **Account No** field. This completes the data you need to enter into the General Journal dialog box to record the compound journal entry for the initial investment by the owner. Your screen should look like this:

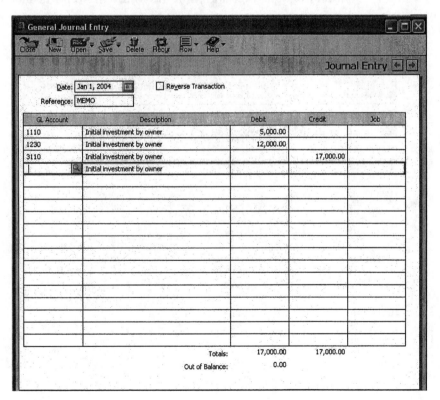

Review the Compound Journal Entry

9. Review the compound journal entry for accuracy, noting any errors and making any editing corrections required.

10. After verifying that the compound journal entry is correct, click on the **Save** icon to post this transaction.

Record Additional Transactions

11. Record the following additional journal entries Enter the **Date** listed for each transaction (you may use the "+" key to advance the date or use the calendar icon next to the field to select the date from a calendar). Enter "MEMO" into the **Reference** text box for each transaction or accept Peachtree's additional number added to MEMO by pressing TAB:

2004

Jan.		
	1	Paid rent for two months in advance, $500.
	3	Purchased office supplies ($200) and office equipment ($1,100) both on account. (compound journal entry). Be sure to use the asset accounts.
	9	Billed a customer for fees earned, $2,000.
	13	Paid telephone bill, $150.
	20	Owner withdrew $475 from the business for personal use.
	27	Received $600 for fees earned.
	31	Paid salaries expense, $800.

Display and Print a General Journal and Trial Balance

12. After you have posted the additional journal entries, close the General Journal dialogue box and print the following reports accepting all defaults:

a. General Journal (Totals = 22,825.00)

The Zell Company-Student Name
General Journal
For the Period From Jan 1, 2004 to Jan 31, 2004

Filter Criteria includes: Report order is by Date. Report is printed with Accounts having Zero Amounts and with Truncated Transaction Descriptions and in Detail Format.

Date	Account ID	Reference	Trans Description	Debit Amt	Credit Amt
1/1/04	1110	MEMO	Initial investment by owner	5,000.00	
	1230		Initial investment by owner	12,000.00	
	3110		Initial investment by owner		17,000.00
1/1/04	1140	MEMO1	Pre-paid rent	500.00	
	1110		Pre-paid rent		500.00
1/3/04	1150	MEMO2	Purchase office supplies and equipment	200.00	
	1210		Purchase office supplies and equipment	1,100.00	
	2110		Purchase office supplies and equipment		1,300.00
1/9/04	4110	MEMO3	Billed customer for fees earned		2,000.00
	1120		Billed customer for fees earned	2,000.00	
1/13/04	5150	MEMO4	Paid telephone bill	150.00	
	1110		Paid telephone bill		150.00
1/20/04	3120	MEMO5	Owner Withdrawal	475.00	
	1110		Owner Withdrawal		475.00
1/27/04	1110	MEMO6	Fees earned	600.00	
	4110		Fees earned		600.00
1/31/04	5120	MEMO7	Paid salaries	800.00	
	1110		Paid salaries		800.00
		Total		22,825.00	22,825.00

b. General Ledger Trial Balance (Totals = 20,900)

Filter Criteria includes: Report order is by ID. Report is printed in Detail Format.

Account ID	Account Description	Debit Amt	Credit Amt
1110	Cash	3,675.00	
1120	Accounts Receivable	2,000.00	
1140	Prepaid Rent	500.00	
1150	Office Supplies	200.00	
1210	Office Equipment	1,100.00	
1230	Automobile	12,000.00	
2110	Accounts Payable		1,300.00
3110	Owner's Capital		17,000.00
3120	Owner's Withdrawals	475.00	
4110	Fees Earned		2,600.00
5120	Salaries Expense	800.00	
5150	Telephone Expense	150.00	
	Total:	20,900.00	20,900.00

13. Review your printed reports. If you have made an error in a posted journal entry you can zoom in on the entry and make the necessary corrections following the instructions given in Chapter 1 for correcting an entry.

How to Record Adjusting Journal Entries

14. Open the General Journal Entry dialogue box; then record adjusting journal entries based on the following adjustment data (*Date:* 1/31/04; *Reference:* ADJ). You may enter all of the adjustments on the same page before posting (see the screen capture below):

a. One month's rent has expired.
b. An inventory shows $25 of office supplies remaining.
c. Depreciation on office equipment, $50.
d. Depreciation on automobile, $150.

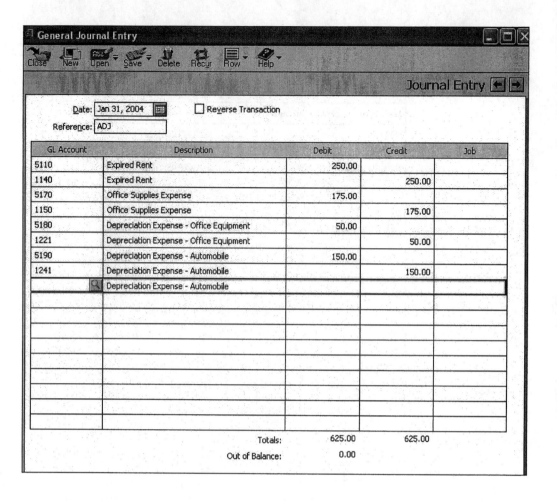

Display and Print a General Journal, General Ledger, and Trial Balance

15. After you have posted the adjusting journal entries, close the General Journal Entry dialogue box and print the following reports from the **General Ledger** option of the **Reports** menu:

   a. General Journal

Date	Account ID	Reference	Trans Description	Debit Amt	Credit Amt
1/1/04	1110	MEMO	Initial investment by owner	5,000.00	
	1230		Initial investment by owner	12,000.00	
	3110		Initial investment by owner		17,000.00
1/1/04	1140	MEMO1	Pre-paid rent	500.00	
	1110		Pre-paid rent		500.00
1/3/04	1150	MEMO2	Purchase office supplies and equipment	200.00	
	1210		Purchase office supplies and equipment	1,100.00	
	2110		Purchase office supplies and equipment		1,300.00
1/9/04	4110	MEMO3	Billed customer for fees earned		2,000.00
	1120		Billed customer for fees earned	2,000.00	
1/13/04	5150	MEMO4	Paid telephone bill	150.00	
	1110		Paid telephone bill		150.00
1/20/04	3120	MEMO5	Owner Withdrawal	475.00	
	1110		Owner Withdrawal		475.00
1/27/04	1110	MEMO6	Fees earned	600.00	
	4110		Fees earned		600.00
1/31/04	5110	ADJ	Expired Rent	250.00	
	1140		Expired Rent		250.00
	5170		Office Supplies Expense	175.00	
	1150		Office Supplies Expense		175.00
	5180		Depreciation Expense - Office Equipment	50.00	
	1221		Depreciation Expense - Office Equipment		50.00

b. General Ledger Report

The Zell Company-Student Name
General Ledger
For the Period From Jan 1, 2004 to Jan 31, 2004
Filter Criteria includes: Report order is by ID. Report is printed with Truncated Transaction Descriptions and in Detail Format.

Account ID Account Description	Date	Reference	Jrnl	Trans Description	Debit Amt	Credit Amt	Balance
1110	1/1/04			Beginning Balance			
Cash	1/1/04	MEMO	GENJ	Initial investment by o	5,000.00		
	1/1/04	MEMO1	GENJ	Pre-paid rent		500.00	
	1/13/04	MEMO4	GENJ	Paid telephone bill		150.00	
	1/20/04	MEMO5	GENJ	Owner Withdrawal		475.00	
	1/27/04	MEMO6	GENJ	Fees earned	600.00		
	1/31/04	MEMO7	GENJ	Paid salaries		800.00	
				Current Period Change	5,600.00	1,925.00	3,675.00
	1/31/04			Ending Balance			3,675.00
1120	1/1/04			Beginning Balance			
Accounts Receivable	1/9/04	MEMO3	GENJ	Billed customer for fee	2,000.00		
				Current Period Change	2,000.00		2,000.00
	1/31/04			Ending Balance			2,000.00
1140	1/1/04			Beginning Balance			
Prepaid Rent	1/1/04	MEMO1	GENJ	Pre-paid rent	500.00		
	1/31/04	ADJ	GENJ	Expired Rent		250.00	
				Current Period Change	500.00	250.00	250.00
	1/31/04			Ending Balance			250.00
1150	1/1/04			Beginning Balance			
Office Supplies	1/3/04	MEMO2	GENJ	Purchase office supplie	200.00		
	1/31/04	ADJ	GENJ	Office Supplies Expens		175.00	
				Current Period Change	200.00	175.00	25.00
	1/31/04			Ending Balance			25.00

c. General Ledger Trial Balance

The Zell Company-Student Name
General Ledger Trial Balance
As of Jan 31, 2004
Filter Criteria includes: Report order is by ID. Report is printed in Detail Format.

Account ID	Account Description	Debit Amt	Credit Amt
1110	Cash	3,675.00	
1120	Accounts Receivable	2,000.00	
1140	Prepaid Rent	250.00	
1150	Office Supplies	25.00	
1210	Office Equipment	1,100.00	
1221	Accum. Depr- Office Equipment		50.00
1230	Automobile	12,000.00	
1241	Accum. Depr- Automobile		150.00
2110	Accounts Payable		1,300.00
3110	Owner's Capital		17,000.00
3120	Owner's Withdrawals	475.00	
4110	Fees Earned		2,600.00
5110	Rent Expense	250.00	
5120	Salaries Expense	800.00	
5150	Telephone Expense	150.00	
5170	Supplies Expense	175.00	
5180	Depr Expense- Office Equipmen	50.00	
5190	Depr Expense- Automobile	150.00	
	Total:	21,100.00	21,100.00

16. Review your printed reports. If you have made an error in a posted journal entry, make the necessary changes and reprint the reports.

17. Select the **Financial Statements** option of the **Reports** menu. Select <Standard> Income Stmnt. An Options dialog box will appear asking you to define the information you want displayed. Press the **OK** button to accept the defaults and display the report on your screen. Your screen will look something like this:

	The Zell Company-Student Name			
	Income Statement			
	For the One Month Ending January 31, 2004			
	Current Month		Year to Date	
Revenues				
Fees Earned	$ 2,600.00	100.00	$ 2,600.00	100.00
Total Revenues	2,600.00	100.00	2,600.00	100.00
Cost of Sales				
Total Cost of Sales	0.00	0.00	0.00	0.00
Gross Profit	2,600.00	100.00	2,600.00	100.00
Expenses				
Rent Expense	250.00	9.62	250.00	9.62
Salaries Expense	800.00	30.77	800.00	30.77
Telephone Expense	150.00	5.77	150.00	5.77
Supplies Expense	175.00	6.73	175.00	6.73
Depr Expense- Office Equipment	50.00	1.92	50.00	1.92
Depr Expense- Automobile	150.00	5.77	150.00	5.77
Total Expenses	1,575.00	60.58	1,575.00	60.58
Net Income	$ 1,025.00	39.42	$ 1,025.00	39.42

18. The scroll bars can be used to advance the display to view other portions of the report as needed.

19. Click on the **Print** icon to print the Income Statement. Close the Income Statement window. This should return you to the Select a Report dialogue box.

20. Select <Standard> Balance Sheet. An Options dialog box will appear asking you to define the information you want displayed. Press the **OK** button to accept the defaults and display the report on your screen. Your screen will look something like this:

```
                                              The Zell Company-Student Name
                                                    Balance Sheet
                                                   January 31, 2004

                                                       ASSETS

Current Assets
Cash                               $         3,675.00
Accounts Receivable                          2,000.00
Prepaid Rent                                   250.00
Office Supplies                                 25.00
                                        _____

Total Current Assets                                              5,950.00

Property and Equipment
Office Equipment                             1,100.00
Accum. Depr- Office Equipment                  (50.00)
Automobile                                  12,000.00
Accum. Depr- Automobile                       (150.00)
                                        _____

Total Property and Equipment                                    12,900.00

Other Assets
                                        _____

Total Other Assets                                                   0.00

Total Assets                       $                             18,850.00
```

21. Use the scroll bars to advance the display to the Owner's Equity section of the Balance Sheet. Note that the program has included the Statement of Owner's Equity information directly in the Owner's Equity section of the Balance Sheet.

22. Click on Print to print the Balance Sheet and then close the Balance Sheet window.

How to Save your Work During a Current Work Session

23. There is no need to save your work in Peachtree. Each time you make a change and click save, your work is automatically saved.

24. You should back up your work after each session following the instructions in Chapter 1.

Exit from the Program

25. Click on the **File** menu; then click on **Exit** to end the current work session and return to your Windows desktop. Your work will automatically be saved.

PEACHTREE
Workshop

CHAPTER 4

The Closing Process - Valdez Realty Mini Practice Set

Before starting on this assignment, read and complete Chapter 1 and 2.

This comprehensive review problem requires you to complete the accounting cycle for Valdez Realty twice. This will allow you to review Chapters 1-2 while reinforcing the relationships between all parts of the accounting cycle. By completing two cycles, you will see how the ending June balances in the ledger which are used to accumulate data in July.

PART A: The June Accounting Cycle

On June 1, Juan Valdez opened a real estate office called Valdez Realty.

Open the Company Data Files

1. Open the software program by double clicking on the Peachtree Complete 2005 icon on your desktop.

2. Open the **Valdez Realty** company data file.

    You should back up your work before starting each chapter following instructions in Chapter 1.

How to Add Your Name to the Company Name

3. Click on the **Maintain** menu option. Then select **Company Information**. The program will respond by bringing up a dialogue box allowing the user to edit/add information about the company.

4. Click in the **Company Name** entry field at the end of **Valdez Realty**. Add a dash and your name "**-Student Name**". Click on the **OK** button to return to the Menu Window.

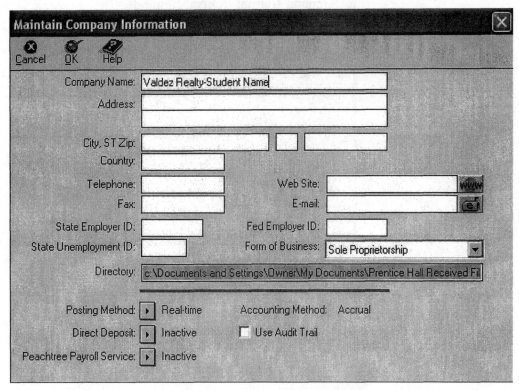

Maintain Company Information

Cancel   OK   Help

Company Name: Valdez Realty-Student Name

Address:

City, ST Zip:

Country:

Telephone: Web Site:

Fax: E-mail:

State Employer ID: Fed Employer ID:

State Unemployment ID: Form of Business: Sole Proprietorship

Directory: c:\Documents and Settings\Owner\My Documents\Prentice Hall Received Fil

Posting Method: ▶ Real-time   Accounting Method: Accrual

Direct Deposit: ▶ Inactive   ☐ Use Audit Trail

Peachtree Payroll Service: ▶ Inactive

Record June Transactions

5. Record the following journal entries. Enter the **Date** listed for each transaction. Enter "MEMO" into the **Reference** text box for each transaction or accept Peachtree's additional number added to memo by pressing TAB:

> 2004
> Jun.
> 1 Juan Valdez invested $7,000 cash in the real estate agency along with $3,000 in office equipment.
> 1 Rented office space and paid three months' rent in advance, $2,100.
> 1 Bought an automobile on account, $12,000.
> 4 Purchased office supplies for cash, $300.
> 5 Purchased additional office supplies on account, $150.
> 6 Sold a house and collected a $6,000 commission.
> 8 Paid gas bill, $22.
> 15 Paid the salary of the office secretary, $350.
> 17 Sold a building lot and earned a commission, $6,500. Expected receipt 7/8/04.
> 20 Juan Valdez withdrew $1,000 from the business to pay personal expenses.
> 21 Sold a house and collected a $3,500 commission.
> 22 Paid gas bill, $25.
> 24 Paid $600 to repair automobile.
> 30 Paid the salary of the office secretary, $350.
> 30 Paid the June telephone bill, $510.
> 30 Received advertising bill for June, $1,200. The bill is to be paid on 7/2/04.

Print Working Reports

6. After you have posted the journal entries, close the General Journal; then print the following reports:

a. General Journal -(check figure debit = $44,607)

			Valdez Realty-Student Name		
			General Journal		
			For the Period From Jun 1, 2004 to Jun 30, 2004		
			Filter Criteria includes: Report order is by Date. Report is printed with Accounts having Zero Amounts and with Truncated Transaction Descriptions and in Detail Format.		

Date	Account ID	Reference	Trans Description	Debit Amt	Credit Amt
6/1/04	1110	MEMO	Owner Investment	7,000.00	
	1210		Owner Investment	3,000.00	
	3110		Owner Investment		10,000.00
6/1/04	1140	MEMO1	Prepaid 3 months rent	2,100.00	
	1110		Prepaid 3 months rent		2,100.00
6/1/04	1230	MEMO2	Purchased automobile	12,000.00	
	2110		Purchased automobile		12,000.00
6/4/04	1150	MEMO3	Purchased office supplies	300.00	
	1110		Purchased office supplies		300.00
6/5/04	1150	MEMO4	Purchased office supplies on account	150.00	
	2110		Purchased office supplies on account		150.00
6/6/04	1110	MEMO5	Received commission on sale of house	6,000.00	
	4110		Received commission on sale of house		6,000.00
6/8/04	5130	MEMO6	Paid gas bill	22.00	
	1110		Paid gas bill		22.00
6/15/04	5120	MEMO7	Paid salary of office secretary	350.00	
	1110		Paid salary of office secretary		350.00
6/17/04	1120	MEMO8	Earned commission on sale of house	6,500.00	
	4110		Earned commission on sale of house		6,500.00
6/20/04	3120	MEMO9	Owner withdrawal	1,000.00	
	1110		Owner withdrawal		1,000.00
6/21/04	1110	MEMO10	Received commission on sale of house	3,500.00	

b. Trial Balance -(Check figure = $39,350)

		Valdez Realty-Student Name	
		General Ledger Trial Balance	
		As of Jun 30, 2004	
	Filter Criteria includes: Report order is by ID. Report is printed in Detail Format.		

Account ID	Account Description	Debit Amt	Credit Amt
1110	Cash	11,243.00	
1120	Accounts Receivable	6,500.00	
1140	Prepaid Rent	2,100.00	
1150	Office Supplies	450.00	
1210	Office Equipment	3,000.00	
1230	Automobile	12,000.00	
2110	Accounts Payable		13,350.00
3110	Juan Valdez, Capital		10,000.00
3120	Juan Valdez Withdrawals	1,000.00	
4110	Commissions Earned		16,000.00
5110	Rent Expense	1,200.00	
5120	Salaries Expense	700.00	
5130	Gas Expense	47.00	
5140	Repairs Expense	600.00	
5150	Telephone Expense	510.00	
	Total:	39,350.00	39,350.00

Review your printed reports. If you have made an error in a posted journal entry, correct the error before proceeding.

7. Open the General Journal; then record adjusting journal entries based on the following adjustment data using "June 30, 2004" as the date and "ADJ JUNE" in the reference field:

   a. One month's rent has expired

   b. An inventory shows $50 of office supplies remaining.

   c. Depreciation on office equipment, $100

   d. Depreciation on automobile, $200

8. After you have posted the adjusting journal entries, close the General Journal then print the following reports accepting all defaults offered by Peachtree:

   a. General Journal -(check figure = $46,007)

Valdez Realty-Student Name
General Journal
For the Period From Jun 1, 2004 to Jun 30, 2004
Filter Criteria includes: Report order is by Date. Report is printed with Accounts having Zero Amounts and with Truncated Transaction Descriptions and i

Date	Account ID	Reference	Trans Description	Debit Amt	Credit Amt
6/1/04	1110	MEMO	Owner Investment	7,000.00	
	1210		Owner Investment	3,000.00	
	3110		Owner Investment		10,000.00
6/1/04	1140	MEMO1	Prepaid 3 months rent	2,100.00	
	1110		Prepaid 3 months rent		2,100.00
6/1/04	1230	MEMO2	Purchased automobile	12,000.00	
	2110		Purchased automobile		12,000.00
6/4/04	1150	MEMO3	Purchased office supplies	300.00	
	1110		Purchased office supplies		300.00
6/5/04	1150	MEMO4	Purchased office supplies on account	150.00	
	2110		Purchased office supplies on account		150.00
6/6/04	1110	MEMO5	Received commission on sale of house	6,000.00	
	4110		Received commission on sale of house		6,000.00
6/8/04	5130	MEMO6	Paid gas bill	22.00	
	1110		Paid gas bill		22.00
6/15/04	5120	MEMO7	Paid salary of office secretary	350.00	
	1110		Paid salary of office secretary		350.00
6/17/04	1120	MEMO8	Earned commission on sale of house	6,500.00	
	4110		Earned commission on sale of house		6,500.00
6/20/04	3120	MEMO9	Owner withdrawal	1,000.00	
	1110		Owner withdrawal		1,000.00

   b. Trial Balance -(check figure = $39,650)

```
                                              Valdez Realty-Student Name
                                            General Ledger Trial Balance
                                                  As of Jun 30, 2004
Filter Criteria includes: Report order is by ID. Report is printed in Detail Format.

Account ID    Account Description            Debit Amt      Credit Amt

1110          Cash                           11,243.00
1120          Accounts Receivable             6,500.00
1140          Prepaid Rent                    1,400.00
1150          Office Supplies                    50.00
1210          Office Equipment                3,000.00
1221          Accum. Depr- Office Equipment                    100.00
1230          Automobile                     12,000.00
1241          Accum. Depr- Automobile                          200.00
2110          Accounts Payable                              13,350.00
3110          Juan Valdez, Capital                          10,000.00
3120          Juan Valdez Withdrawals         1,000.00
4110          Commissions Earned                            16,000.00
5110          Rent Expense                    1,900.00
5120          Salaries Expense                  700.00
5130          Gas Expense                        47.00
5140          Repairs Expense                   600.00
5150          Telephone Expense                 510.00
5170          Office Supplies Expense           400.00
5180          Depr Expense- Office Equipmen     100.00
5190          Depr Expense- Automobile          200.00

              Total:                         39,650.00      39,650.00
```

c. General Ledger Report -(check figure cash = $11,243)

```
                                              Valdez Realty-Student Name
                                                  General Ledger
                                       For the Period From Jun 1, 2004 to Jun 30, 2004
Filter Criteria includes: Report order is by ID. Report is printed with Truncated Transaction Descriptions and in Detail Format.

Account ID       Date      Reference   Jrnl   Trans Description      Debit Amt   Credit Amt   Balance
Account Description

1110             6/1/04                        Beginning Balance
Cash             6/1/04    MEMO        GENJ    Owner Investment       7,000.00
                 6/1/04    MEMO1       GENJ    Prepaid 3 months rent              2,100.00
                 6/4/04    MEMO3       GENJ    Purchased office suppli             300.00
                 6/6/04    MEMO5       GENJ    Received commission    6,000.00
                 6/8/04    MEMO6       GENJ    Paid gas bill                         22.00
                 6/15/04   MEMO7       GENJ    Paid salary of office se            350.00
                 6/20/04   MEMO9       GENJ    Owner withdrawal                  1,000.00
                 6/21/04   MEMO10      GENJ    Received commission    3,500.00
                 6/22/04   MEMO11      GENJ    Paid gas bill                         25.00
                 6/24/04   MEMO12      GENJ    Automobile repair                   600.00
                 6/30/04   MEMO13      GENJ    Paid salary of office se            350.00
                 6/30/04   MEMO14      GENJ    Paid telephone bill                 510.00
                                               Current Period Change  16,500.00   5,257.00   11,243.00
                 6/30/04                        Ending Balance                               11,243.00


1120             6/1/04                        Beginning Balance
Accounts Receivable  6/17/04  MEMO8    GENJ    Earned commission on   6,500.00
                                               Current Period Change  6,500.00              6,500.00
                 6/30/04                        Ending Balance                               6,500.00


1140             6/1/04                        Beginning Balance
Prepaid Rent     6/1/04    MEMO1       GENJ    Prepaid 3 months rent  2,100.00
                 6/30/04   ADJ JUNE    GENJ    Adjusting Entries for J             700.00
                                               Current Period Change  2,100.00    700.00    1,400.00
                 6/30/04                        Ending Balance                               1,400.00
```

d. Income Statement -(Net Income = $11,543)

Valdez Realty-Student Name
Income Statement
For the Six Months Ending June 30, 2004

	Current Month		Year to Date	
Revenues				
Commissions Earned	$ 16,000.00	100.00	$ 16,000.00	100.00
Total Revenues	16,000.00	100.00	16,000.00	100.00
Cost of Sales				
Total Cost of Sales	0.00	0.00	0.00	0.00
Gross Profit	16,000.00	100.00	16,000.00	100.00
Expenses				
Rent Expense	1,900.00	11.88	1,900.00	11.88
Salaries Expense	700.00	4.38	700.00	4.38
Gas Expense	47.00	0.29	47.00	0.29
Repairs Expense	600.00	3.75	600.00	3.75
Telephone Expense	510.00	3.19	510.00	3.19
Advertising Expense	0.00	0.00	0.00	0.00
Office Supplies Expense	400.00	2.50	400.00	2.50
Depr Expense- Office Equipment	100.00	0.63	100.00	0.63
Depr Expense- Automobile	200.00	1.25	200.00	1.25
Miscellaneous Expense	0.00	0.00	0.00	0.00
Total Expenses	4,457.00	27.86	4,457.00	27.86
Net Income	$ 11,543.00	72.14	$ 11,543.00	72.14

e. Balance Sheet -(Total Assets = $33,893)

```
                                           Valdez Realty-Student Name
                                                 Balance Sheet
                                                 June 30, 2004

                                                      ASSETS

Current Assets
Cash                                  $        11,243.00
Accounts Receivable                             6,500.00
Prepaid Rent                                    1,400.00
Office Supplies                                    50.00

Total Current Assets                                              19,193.00

Property and Equipment
Office Equipment                                3,000.00
Accum. Depr- Office Equipment                    (100.00)
Automobile                                     12,000.00
Accum. Depr- Automobile                          (200.00)

Total Property and Equipment                                     14,700.00

Other Assets

Total Other Assets                                                    0.00

Total Assets                          $                           33,893.00


                                              LIABILITIES AND CAPITAL

Current Liabilities
Accounts Payable                      $        13,350.00

Total Current Liabilities                                        13,350.00
```

Review your printed reports. If you have made an error in a posted journal entry make any necessary corrections. Reprint all reports if corrections are made.

Closing the Accounting Records

9. Computerized Accounting systems maintain all of its input in compartments called periods. Some systems identify these periods with the name of the month or with a simple numeric designation such as 1, 2, 3, et. al. Peachtree currently has Valdez Realty in Period 6, the June period. You can see this in the status bar at the bottom of the screen. This is because Valdez has elected to use the calendar year for his Fiscal year. We will need to change the current period to the July period prior to inputting the July transactions in part B of this workshop. You must always tell Peachtree to move to the next accounting period when starting on the transactions for a new month. This process is the equivalent of "Closing" in a manual accounting system although the temporary accounts are not really closed until the end of the year.

Make a Backup Copy of June Accounting

10. It is always wise to backup accounting data at the end of each month, saving it into a file that will be saved until the end of the year. Click on the Company Window **File** menu; select **Backup** Be sure to include the company name and add "EndJun" to make sure you can recognize what the backup represents. Click **Ok**.

Advancing the Period

11. We must now advance the period to prepare Peachtree for the July transactions.

   ♦ Click on **System** from the **Tasks** menu. Select **Change Accounting Periods**. You are presented with the following:

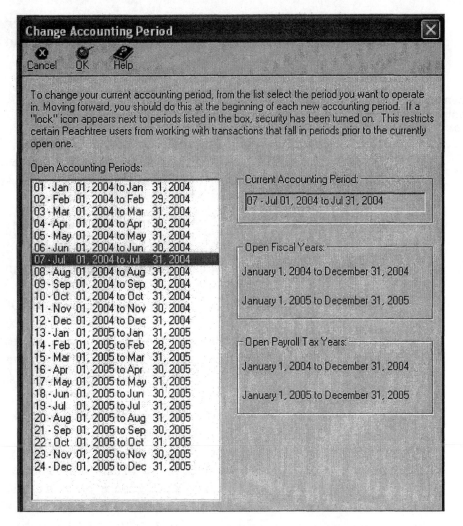

- Using the list at left, select 07- Jul 1, 2004 to Jul 31, 2004 and click on **O**k

- You will be asked whether you wish to print reports before continuing. Since we have already printed our reports, click "No".

- Note that the status bar at the bottom of the screen now reflects that you are in period 7.

**Exit the
Program**

12. Click on the Company Window File menu; then click on Exit to end the current work session and return to your Windows desktop or continue with step 3 below in Part B.

Open the Company Data Files

1. Start Peachtree Complete Accounting 2005.

2. Open the existing company file for **Valdez Realty.**

3. Record the following journal entries. Enter the **Date** listed for each transaction. Enter "MEMO" into the **Reference** text box and accept Peachtree's additional number added to memo by pressing TAB:

Record July Transactions

2004

Jul.	1	Purchased additional office supplies on account, $700.
	2	Paid advertising bill for June, $1200.
	3	Sold a house and collected a commission, $6,600.
	6	Paid for gas expense, $29.
	8	Collected commission from sale of building lot on 6/17/04 (collected our accounts receivable).
	12	Paid $300 to send employees to realtor's workshop.
	15	Paid the salary of the office secretary, $350.
	17	Sold a house and earned a commission of $2,400. Expected receipt on 8/10/04.
	18	Sold a building lot and collected a commission of $7,000.
	22	Sent a check for $40 to help sponsor a local road race to aid the public (This is not to be considered an advertising expense, but it is a business expense.)
	24	Paid for repairs to automobile, $590.
	28	Juan Valdez withdrew $1,800 from the business to pay personal expenses.
	30	Paid the salary of the office secretary, $350.
	30	Paid the July telephone bill, $590.
	30	Advertising bill for July, $1,400. The bill is to be paid on 8/2/04.

Print Working Reports

4. After you have posted the journal entries, close the General Journal; then print the following reports:

a. General Journal -(check figure debit = $29,849)

Valdez Realty-Student Name
General Journal
For the Period From Jul 1, 2004 to Jul 31, 2004
Filter Criteria includes: Report order is by Date. Report is printed with Accounts having Zero Amounts and with Truncated Transaction Descriptions and in Detail Format

Date	Account ID	Reference	Trans Description	Debit Amt	Credit Amt
7/1/04	1150	MEMO	Purchased office supplies	700.00	
	2110		Purchased office supplies		700.00
7/2/04	2110	MEMO1	Paid the advertising bill in accounts payable	1,200.00	
	1110		Paid the advertising bill in accounts payable		1,200.00
7/3/04	1110	MEMO2	Received commission on sale of house	6,600.00	
	4110		Received commission on sale of house		6,600.00
7/6/04	5130	MEMO3	Paid gas bill	29.00	
	1110		Paid gas bill		29.00
7/8/04	1110	MEMO4	Collected commission in accounts receivabl	6,500.00	
	1120		Collected commission in accounts receivabl		6,500.00
7/12/04	5200	MEMO5	Workshop for employees	300.00	
	1110		Workshop for employees		300.00
7/15/04	5120	MEMO6	Paid salary of office secretary	350.00	
	1110		Paid salary of office secretary		350.00
7/17/04	1120	MEMO7	Commission on sale of house	2,400.00	
	4110		Commission on sale of house		2,400.00
7/18/04	1110	MEMO8	Commission on sale of house	7,000.00	
	4110		Commission on sale of house		7,000.00
7/22/04	5200	MEMO9	Sponsor a local road race to aid public	40.00	
	1110		Sponsor a local road race to aid public		40.00

b. Trial Balance -(Check figure debit = $56,550)

Account ID	Account Description	Debit Amt	Credit Amt
1110	Cash	26,094.00	
1120	Accounts Receivable	2,400.00	
1140	Prepaid Rent	1,400.00	
1150	Office Supplies	750.00	
1210	Office Equipment	3,000.00	
1221	Accum. Depr- Office Equipment		100.00
1230	Automobile	12,000.00	
1241	Accum. Depr- Automobile		200.00
2110	Accounts Payable		14,250.00
3110	Juan Valdez, Capital		10,000.00
3120	Juan Valdez Withdrawals	2,800.00	
4110	Commissions Earned		32,000.00
5110	Rent Expense	1,900.00	
5120	Salaries Expense	1,400.00	
5130	Gas Expense	76.00	
5140	Repairs Expense	1,190.00	
5150	Telephone Expense	1,100.00	
5160	Advertising Expense	1,400.00	
5170	Office Supplies Expense	400.00	
5180	Depr Expense- Office Equipmen	100.00	
5190	Depr Expense- Automobile	200.00	
5200	Miscellaneous Expense	340.00	
	Total:	56,550.00	56,550.00

Review your printed reports. If you have made an error in a posted journal entry, correct the error before proceeding. Reprint the reports if necessary.

Record July Adjusting Entries

5. Open the General Journal; then record adjusting journal entries based on the following adjustment data using July 31, 2004 as the date and "ADJ JULY" in the reference field:

a. One month's rent has expired.

b. An inventory shows $90 of office supplies remaining.

c. Depreciation on office equipment, $100.

d. Depreciation on automobile, $200.

Print Final Statements

6. After you have posted the adjusting journal entries, close the General Journal then print the following reports accepting all defaults offered by Peachtree:

a. General Journal -(check figure = $31,509)

Valdez Realty-Student Name
General Journal
For the Period From Jul 1, 2004 to Jul 31, 2004
Filter Criteria includes: Report order is by Date. Report is printed with Accounts having Zero Amounts and with Truncated Transaction Descriptions and in Deta

Date	Account ID	Reference	Trans Description	Debit Amt	Credit Amt
7/12/04	5200	MEMO5	Workshop for employees	300.00	
	1110		Workshop for employees		300.00
7/15/04	5120	MEMO6	Paid salary of office secretary	350.00	
	1110		Paid salary of office secretary		350.00
7/17/04	1120	MEMO7	Commission on sale of house	2,400.00	
	4110		Commission on sale of house		2,400.00
7/18/04	1110	MEMO8	Commission on sale of house	7,000.00	
	4110		Commission on sale of house		7,000.00
7/22/04	5200	MEMO9	Sponsor a local road race to aid public	40.00	
	1110		Sponsor a local road race to aid public		40.00
7/24/04	5140	MEMO10	Repairs to automobile	590.00	
	1110		Repairs to automobile		590.00
7/28/04	3120	MEMO11	Owner withdrawal	1,800.00	
	1110		Owner withdrawal		1,800.00
7/30/04	5120	MEMO12	Paid salary of office secretary	350.00	
	1110		Paid salary of office secretary		350.00
7/30/04	5150	MEMO13	Paid telephone bill	590.00	
	1110		Paid telephone bill		590.00
7/30/04	5160	MEMO14	Advertising	1,400.00	
	2110		Advertising		1,400.00
			Total	31,509.00	31,509.00

b. Trial Balance -(check figure = $56,850)

Valdez Realty-Student Name
General Ledger Trial Balance
As of Jul 31, 2004
Filter Criteria includes: Report order is by ID. Report is printed in Detail Format.

Account ID	Account Description	Debit Amt	Credit Amt
1110	Cash	26,094.00	
1120	Accounts Receivable	2,400.00	
1140	Prepaid Rent	700.00	
1150	Office Supplies	90.00	
1210	Office Equipment	3,000.00	
1221	Accum. Depr- Office Equipment		200.00
1230	Automobile	12,000.00	
1241	Accum. Depr- Automobile		400.00
2110	Accounts Payable		14,250.00
3110	Juan Valdez, Capital		10,000.00
3120	Juan Valdez Withdrawals	2,800.00	
4110	Commissions Earned		32,000.00
5110	Rent Expense	2,600.00	
5120	Salaries Expense	1,400.00	
5130	Gas Expense	76.00	
5140	Repairs Expense	1,190.00	
5150	Telephone Expense	1,100.00	
5160	Advertising Expense	1,400.00	
5170	Office Supplies Expense	1,060.00	
5180	Depr Expense- Office Equipmen	200.00	
5190	Depr Expense- Automobile	400.00	
5200	Miscellaneous Expense	340.00	
	Total:	56,850.00	56,850.00

c. General Ledger Report -(check figure cash = $26,094)

Valdez Realty-Student Name
General Ledger
For the Period From Jul 1, 2004 to Jul 31, 2004
Filter Criteria includes: Report order is by ID. Report is printed with Truncated Transaction Descriptions and in Detail Format.

Account ID Account Description	Date	Reference	Jrnl	Trans Description	Debit Amt	Credit Amt	Balance
1110	7/1/04			Beginning Balance			11,243.00
Cash	7/2/04	MEMO1	GENJ	Paid the advertising bil		1,200.00	
	7/3/04	MEMO2	GENJ	Received commission	6,600.00		
	7/6/04	MEMO3	GENJ	Paid gas bill		29.00	
	7/8/04	MEMO4	GENJ	Collected commission	6,500.00		
	7/12/04	MEMO5	GENJ	Workshop for employ		300.00	
	7/15/04	MEMO6	GENJ	Paid salary of office se		350.00	
	7/18/04	MEMO8	GENJ	Commission on sale of	7,000.00		
	7/22/04	MEMO9	GENJ	Sponsor a local road ra		40.00	
	7/24/04	MEMO10	GENJ	Repairs to automobile		590.00	
	7/28/04	MEMO11	GENJ	Owner withdrawal		1,800.00	
	7/30/04	MEMO12	GENJ	Paid salary of office se		350.00	
	7/30/04	MEMO13	GENJ	Paid telephone bill		590.00	
				Current Period Change	20,100.00	5,249.00	14,851.00
	7/31/04			Ending Balance			26,094.00
1120	7/1/04			Beginning Balance			6,500.00
Accounts Receivable	7/8/04	MEMO4	GENJ	Collected commission		6,500.00	
	7/17/04	MEMO7	GENJ	Commission on sale of	2,400.00		
				Current Period Change	2,400.00	6,500.00	-4,100.00
	7/31/04			Ending Balance			2,400.00
1140	7/1/04			Beginning Balance			1,400.00
Prepaid Rent	7/1/04	ADJ JULY	GENJ	July adjusting entries		700.00	
				Current Period Change		700.00	-700.00
	7/31/04			Ending Balance			700.00

d. Income Statement -(Net Income = $10,691)

	Current Month			Year to Date	
Revenues					
Commissions Earned	$ 16,000.00	100.00	$	32,000.00	100.00
Total Revenues	16,000.00	100.00		32,000.00	100.00
Cost of Sales					
Total Cost of Sales	0.00	0.00		0.00	0.00
Gross Profit	16,000.00	100.00		32,000.00	100.00
Expenses					
Rent Expense	700.00	4.38		2,600.00	8.13
Salaries Expense	700.00	4.38		1,400.00	4.38
Gas Expense	29.00	0.18		76.00	0.24
Repairs Expense	590.00	3.69		1,190.00	3.72
Telephone Expense	590.00	3.69		1,100.00	3.44
Advertising Expense	1,400.00	8.75		1,400.00	4.38
Office Supplies Expense	660.00	4.13		1,060.00	3.31
Depr Expense- Office Equipment	100.00	0.63		200.00	0.63
Depr Expense- Automobile	200.00	1.25		400.00	1.25
Miscellaneous Expense	340.00	2.13		340.00	1.06
Total Expenses	5,309.00	33.18		9,766.00	30.52
Net Income	$ 10,691.00	66.82	$	22,234.00	69.48

e. Balance Sheet -(Total Capital = $29,434)

```
                                            Valdez Realty-Student Name
                                                  Balance Sheet
                                                  July 31, 2004

Office Equipment                    3,000.00
Accum. Depr- Office Equipment        (200.00)
Automobile                         12,000.00
Accum. Depr- Automobile              (400.00)

Total Property and Equipment                      14,400.00

Other Assets
                              _____
Total Other Assets                                    0.00
                              _____
Total Assets                              $        43,684.00


                                            LIABILITIES AND CAPITAL

Current Liabilities
Accounts Payable              $    14,250.00

Total Current Liabilities                         14,250.00

Long-Term Liabilities
                              _____
Total Long-Term Liabilities                           0.00
                              _____
Total Liabilities                                 14,250.00

Capital
Juan Valdez, Capital               10,000.00
Juan Valdez Withdrawals            (2,800.00)
Net Income                         22,234.00
```

Review your printed reports. If you have made an error in a posted journal entry, use the procedures detailed in step 18 from chapter 1 to make any necessary corrections. Reprint all reports if corrections are made.

Closing the Accounting Records

7. Peachtree currently has Valdez Realty in Period 7, the July period. You can see this in the status bar at the bottom of the screen. We will need to change the current period to the August period prior to inputting the next month's transactions.

Make a Backup Copy of July Accounting

8. Before changing the period we need to backup our data. Go to **File** menu; select **Backup**. Be sure to include the company name and add "End July" to make sure you can recognize what the backup represents.

Advancing the Period

9. We must now advance the period to prepare Peachtree for the August transactions.

♦ Using your mouse, click on **System** from the **Tasks** menu. Select **Change Accounting Periods**.

♦ Using the pull down menu, select period 8 - Aug 1, 2004 to Aug 31, 2004 and click on **Ok.**

♦ You will be asked whether you wish to print reports before continuing. Since we have already printed our reports select "No".

♦ Note that the status bar at the bottom of the screen now reflects that you are in period 8.

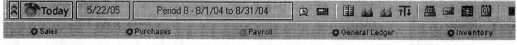

Exit the Program

10. You should back up your file after completing each chapter following the instructions in Chapter 1. Click on the Company Window **File** menu; then click on **Exit** to end the current work session and return to your Windows desktop.

CHAPTER 5

Completing Payroll Requirements for First Quarter - Pete's Market Mini Practice Set

Before starting on this assignment, read and complete Chapters 1 and 2

Pete's Market, owned by Pete Real, is located at 4 Sun Avenue, Swampscott, Massachusetts 01970. His employer identification number is 42-4583312. The version of Peachtree Complete Accounting 2005 used with this text uses the state and federal tax laws in effect for calendar year 2004. Federal Income Tax (FIT), State Income Tax (SIT), Social Security, Medicare, FUTA, and SUTA are all calculated automatically by the program based on the following assumptions and built-in tax rates:

1. FICA: Social Security, 6.2 percent on $84,900; Medicare, 1.45 percent on all earnings.

2. SUTA: 4.9 percent on the first $10,800 in earnings.

3. FUTA: .8 percent on the first $7,000 in earnings.

4. Employees are paid monthly. The payroll is recorded and paid on the last day of each month. The company uses a payroll checking account and the net pay must be transferred to that account as part of the payroll process.

5. FIT is calculated automatically by the program based on the marital status and number of exemptions claimed by each employee. These have been set up already. The tables will accommodate only single and married as they currently exist. In a full version of the program, all statuses would be available. In addition, with the full version of the program, the user would subscribe to Peachtree's Tax Table Service, which would periodically update the tax tables to insure accuracy in the calculations. Since the 2004 tax data is not available, the numbers calculated in this book are not accurate.

6. SIT for Massechusetts is calculated automatically by the program based on the marital status and number of exemptions claimed by each employee.

The Payroll module in Peachtree Complete Accounting 2005 is designed to work with the General Ledger module in an integrated fashion. When transactions are recorded in the Payroll Journal, the program automatically updates the employee records, records the journal entry, and posts all accounts affected in the general ledger.

The following are the employees of Pete's Market and their monthly wages they will earn for the first payroll quarter:

	January	February	March
Fred Flynn	$2,500	$2,590	$3,100
Mary Jones	3,000	3,000	4,000
Lilly Vron	3,200	3,400	4,260

The trial balance for Pete's Market as at 1/1/04 appears below:

		Debits	Credits
1010	Cash	84,964.04	—
1020	Payroll Checking Cash	—	—
2310	FIT Payable	—	1,415.94
2320	SIT Payable	—	535.50
2330	Social Security Tax Payable	—	1,116.00
2335	Medicare Tax Payable	—	261.00
2340	FUTA Payable	—	48.00
2350	SUTA Payable	—	1,587.60
3560	Pete Reel, Capital	—	80,000.00
		84,964.04	84,964.04

Open the Company Data Files

1. Double click on the Peachtree icon on your desktop to open the program.

2. Open the existing company file for **Pete's Market**.

You should back up your work before starting each chapter following instructions in Chapter 1.

Add Your Name to the company Name

3. Click on the **Maintain** menu option. Then select **Company Information**. The program will respond by bringing up a dialogue box allowing the user to edit/add information about the company.

4. Click in the **Company Name** entry field at the end of **Pete's Market**. If it is already highlighted, press the right arrow key. Add a dash and your name "**-Student Name**" Click on the OK button to return to the Menu Window.

Record Payment of December Payroll Liabilities and Taxes

5. Record the payment of last month's payroll liabilities using the General Journal Entry window. Assume an electronic transfer was made out of the Cash account number 1010. Enter the **Date** listed for each transaction. Enter "MEMO" into the **Reference** text box for each transaction or accept Peachtree's additional number added to memo by pressing TAB:

2004
Jan. 15 Record the compound journal entry for the deposit of Social Security, Medicare, and FIT from last month's payroll. (We will not record the payment of state income tax.) 941 Deposit
31 Record the payment of SUTA from last quarter.
31 Record the payment of FUTA tax owed. 940 Deposit

How to Record the Payroll

6. Close the General Journal. Peachtree has two options for paying your employees. Both are available using the payroll navigation aid at the bottom of your screen. If it is not showing go to options menu and select View Navigation Aids.

○ Sales	○ Purchases	○ Payroll	○ General Ledger	○ Inventory

That will bring up the payroll navigation window that looks like this:

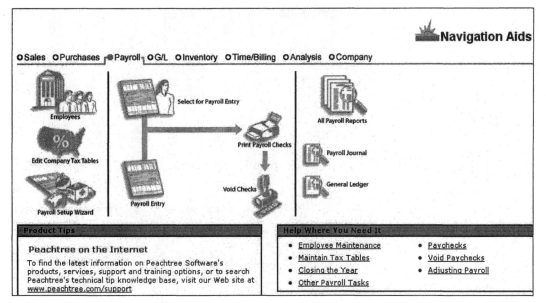

Navigation Aids

○ Sales ○ Purchases ● Payroll ○ G/L ○ Inventory ○ Time/Billing ○ Analysis ○ Company

Employees

Select for Payroll Entry

All Payroll Reports

Print Payroll Checks

Payroll Journal

Edit Company Tax Tables

Void Checks

General Ledger

Payroll Setup Wizard

Payroll Entry

Product Tips

Peachtree on the Internet

To find the latest information on Peachtree Software's products, services, support and training options, or to search Peachtree's technical tip knowledge base, visit our Web site at www.peachtree.com/support

Help Where You Need It

- Employee Maintenance
- Maintain Tax Tables
- Closing the Year
- Other Payroll Tasks

- Paychecks
- Void Paychecks
- Adjusting Payroll

There are two options in the center section of the Navigation Aid. The first option is **Select for Payroll Entry** which selects all employees who meet an indicated criteria while the second, **Payroll Entry**, allows you to select the employees one by one. Since we wish to pay all of our salaried employees, we will select the first option, **Select for Payroll Entry**. This will bring up a dialogue box from which we can filter which employees to pay this period:

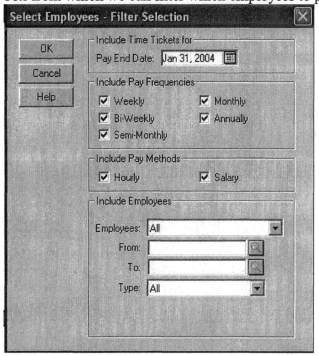

7. Since ours is a monthly payroll paid on the last day of the month, we will change the **Pay End Date:** to reflect January 31 using the small calendar to the right of the field. Click on the small calendar and then select the 31st from the calendar presented. The other filters allow us to pay only a certain frequency type employee, hourly and/or salary, or a range of employees by employee number. You can explore these options but leave them set at the default values shown in the illustration above.

8. Click on the **Ok** button when you are ready to continue. This will bring up a Select Employees to Pay dialogue box:

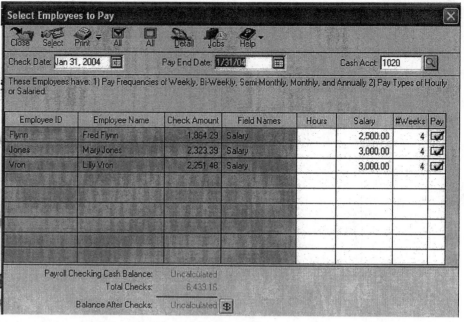

Select Employees to Pay

Close | Select | Print | All | All | Detail | Jobs | Help

Check Date: Jan 31, 2004   Pay End Date: 1/31/04   Cash Acct: 1020

These Employees have: 1) Pay Frequencies of Weekly, Bi-Weekly, Semi-Monthly, Monthly, and Annually 2) Pay Types of Hourly or Salaried.

Employee ID	Employee Name	Check Amount	Field Names	Hours	Salary	#Weeks	Pay
Flynn	Fred Flynn	1,864.29	Salary		2,500.00	4	☑
Jones	Mary Jones	2,323.39	Salary		3,000.00	4	☑
Vron	Lilly Vron	2,251.48	Salary		3,000.00	4	☑

Payroll Checking Cash Balance: Uncalculated

Total Checks: 6,439.16

Balance After Checks: Uncalculated

Review the Payroll

9.   Notice how Peachtree has selected all three of our employees and has automatically flagged them for payment with a red check mark. It has also calculated all of the required withholdings and payroll taxes for each employee. Since we are paying the employees on the last day of the month, we should insure that the **Check Date** reflects January 31, 2004. Also confirm that the **Cash Acct:** is account 1020 Payroll Checking Cash. If it is not, select account 1020 Payroll Checking Cash.

How to Edit a Payroll Journal Entry Prior to Posting

10. If you want to see the detail on any of the employees, simply double click on that employee's entry to bring up a Detail dialogue box. Try selecting Fred Flynn. You can change any of the numbers presented in the white fields of this dialogue box by double clicking on the number you wish to change. We will accept all the information as given. Leave this dialogue box by clicking on **Ok** or **Close** since we made no changes:

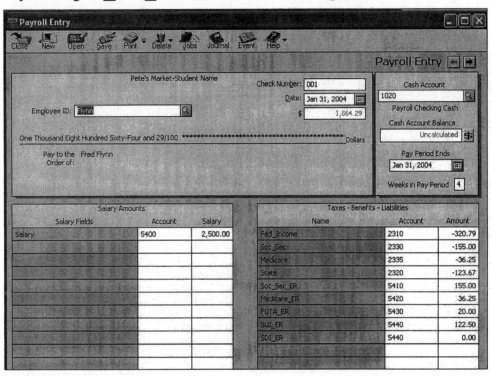

How to Post a Payroll Entry

11. After verifying that the payroll entries are correct, click on the **Print** icon to print checks and post this transaction. A Print Forms: Payroll Checks dialogue box is presented for the user to select the proper check format. Peachtree supports many different blank check formats. Select the first option, "OCR - PR MultiP 2 Stb 15 Flds", since we are printing to a blank sheet of paper and the format will not matter. In a working situation you would determine the correct form to use.

12. You are now prompted for a check number to begin the numbering with. Type in "001" and select **Ok** to print the checks. You may need to tell your printer to continue since it will wait for the user to insert the check forms. Telling it to continue will print the checks on the blank paper. When the checks have finished, you will be asked to confirm the printing process. This feature allows you to print them a second time if something interfered with the printing process the first time through. Upon confirming a successful run, you will be taken back to the Menu Screen of Peachtree and Peachtree will create and post all the necessary journal entries internally.

How to Display and Print a Payroll Register

13. From the **Reports** menu, select **Payroll**. This will bring up a Select a Report dialogue box containing a list of several payroll reports available to us. Select **Payroll Register** to bring up a payroll register for the checks we just issued. We will use this report to determine the net pay for the payroll period. This amount must be transferred to our Payroll Checking account since our paychecks are drawn on that account. It must be funded prior to

issuing the checks to our employees. Accept all defaults provided by Peachtree and we are presented with:

Pete's Market-Student Name
Payroll Register
For the Period From Jan 1, 2004 to Jan 31, 2004
Filter Criteria includes: Report order is by Check Date. Report is printed in Detail Format.

Employee ID Employee SS No Reference Date	Pay Type	Pay Hrs	Pay Amt	Amount	Gross State SUI_ER	Fed_Income Soc_Sec_ER SDI_ER	Soc_Sec Medicare_ER	Medicare FUTA_ER
001 1/31/04					-122.50			
Jones Mary Jones	Salary		3,000.00	2,323.39	3,000.00 -126.32 -147.00	-320.79 -186.00	-186.00 -43.50	-43.50 -24.00
002 1/31/04								
Vron Lilly Vron	Salary		3,000.00	2,251.48	3,000.00 -130.73 -147.00	-388.29 -186.00	-186.00 -43.50	-43.50 -24.00
003 1/31/04								
Summary Total 1/1/04 thru 1/31/04	Salary		8,500.00	6,439.16	8,500.00 -380.72 -416.50	-1,029.87 -527.00	-527.00 -123.25	-123.25 -68.00
Report Date Final Total 1/1/04 thru 1/31/04	Salary		8,500.00	6,439.16	8,500.00 -380.72 -416.50	-1,029.87 -527.00	-527.00 -123.25	-123.25 -68.00

14. We will now transfer cash from our regular Cash account number 1010 into our Payroll Checking account number 1020 in order to cover the checks we have just written. Note from the register totals, we have a total of $6,439.16 in net pay.

  ♦ Select **General Journal Entry** from the **Tasks** menu to open the General Journal dialog box. Enter the date 1/31/04 into the **Date** field; press the TAB key; enter "MEMO" into the **Reference** field and press TAB.

  ♦ Select account number "1020 Payroll Checking Cash"

  ♦ Enter "Transfer net payroll" in the **Description** field

  ♦ Enter "6439.16" in the **Debit** field

  ♦ Tab to **Account No.** and select "1010 Cash"

  ♦ Tab to the **Credit** field and enter "6439.16" again

  ♦ Click **Save** to complete the transfer

Print Reports

15. After you have posted the journal entry, close the General Journal Entry window and print the following reports accepting all defaults offered by Peachtree:

  a. General Journal -(check figure = $10,867.70)

Pete's Market-Student Name
General Journal
For the Period From Jan 1, 2004 to Jan 31, 2004
Filter Criteria includes: Report order is by Date. Report is printed with Accounts having Zero Amounts and with Truncated Transaction Descriptions and in Detail Format.

Date	Account ID	Reference	Trans Description	Debit Amt	Credit Amt
1/15/04	2310	MEMO	941 deposit	1,415.94	
	2330		941 deposit	1,116.00	
	2335		941 deposit	261.00	
	1010		941 deposit		2,792.94
1/31/04	1020	MEMO	Transfer net payroll	6,439.16	
	1010		Transfer net payroll		6,439.16
1/31/04	2350	MEMO1	SUTA payment from 3rd Quarter	1,587.60	
	1010		SUTA payment from 3rd Quarter		1,587.60
1/31/04	2340	MEMO2	FUTA - 940 tax payment	48.00	
	1010		FUTA - 940 tax payment		48.00
		Total		10,867.70	10,867.70

b. Trial Balance -(check figure = $83,748.49)

Account ID	Account Description	Debit Amt	Credit Amt
1010	Cash	74,096.34	
2310	FIT Payable		1,029.87
2320	SIT Payable		916.22
2330	Social Security Tax Payable		1,054.00
2335	Medicare Tax Payable		246.50
2340	FUTA Payable		68.00
2350	SUTA Payable		416.50
3569	Pete Reel, Capital		80,000.00
5400	Wages Expense	8,500.00	
5410	Social Security Tax Expense	527.00	
5420	Medicare Tax Expense	123.25	
5430	FUTA Expense	68.00	
5440	SUTA Expense	416.50	
	Total:	83,731.09	83,731.09

Review your printed reports. If you have made an error in a posted journal entry, make any corrections and reprint all reports.

Make a January Backup Copy

16. It is always wise to backup accounting data at the end of each month, saving it into a file that will be saved until the end of the year. Click on the Company Window **File** menu; select **Backup**, include the company name and add "EndJan" to make sure you can recognize what the backup represents. Click on **Ok**.

Advancing the Period

17. We must now advance the period to prepare Peachtree for the February transactions.

♦ Double click on the period in the Peachtree status bar at the bottom of your screen as shown:

♦ Using the pull down menu, select period 2 - Feb 1, 2004 to Feb 29, 2004 and click on "**Ok**"

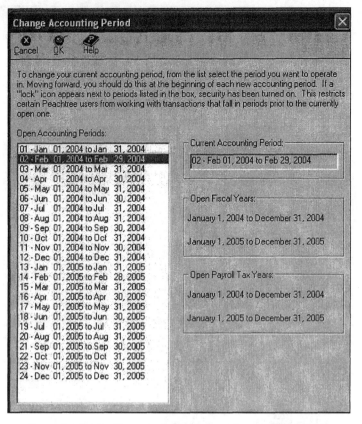

- You may be asked whether you wish to print reports before continuing. Since we have already printed our reports, select "No".

- Note that the status bar at the bottom of the screen now reflects that you are in period 2.

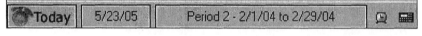

Record Payment of January Payroll Liabilities and

18. Record the following general journal entry using the **date** shown below and "memo" as the **reference number**:

2004

Feb.   16   Record the compound journal entry for the deposit of Social Security, Medicare, and FIT from last month's payroll. Use the trial balance created in #16 above to determine the amounts owed. Total amount to be credited to the cash account 1010 should be $2,330.37.

Record February Payroll

19. Record the February payroll journal entries for Fred Flynn, Mary Jones, and Lilly Vron. Remember that both Fred Flynn and Lilly Vron are making more than their usual amounts this month. Fred will earn $2,590 instead of his usual $2,500 and Lilly will earn $3,400 instead of her usual $3,200. After selecting employees to pay (See How to Record the Payroll above except use February 29), double click on Fred's and Lilly's Salary fields and change their salaries to the new amounts. Everything will automatically recalculate using the new gross. Follow the same procedure for printing checks as you used in January except use the date February 29. Peachtree should select check #004 as the starting check number automatically. Be sure to transfer the net pay into the Payroll Checking Cash account.

Print Reports

20. Print the following reports accepting all defaults:

a. Payroll Register -(check figure Net = $6,733.40)

Employee ID Employee SS No Reference Date	Pay Type	Pay Hrs	Pay Amt	Amount	Gross State SUI_ER	Fed_Income Soc_Sec_ER SDI_ER	Soc_Sec Medicare_ER	Medicare FUTA_ER
Flynn Fred Flynn 004 2/29/04	Salary		2,590.00	1,918.33	2,590.00 -128.44 -126.91	-345.09 -160.58	-160.58 -37.56	-37.56 -20.72
Jones Mary Jones 005 2/29/04	Salary		3,400.00	2,563.59	3,400.00 -147.52 -166.60	-428.79 -210.80	-210.80 -49.30	-49.30 -27.20
Vron Lilly Vron 006 2/29/04	Salary		3,000.00	2,251.48	3,000.00 -130.73 -147.00	-388.29 -186.00	-186.00 -43.50	-43.50 -24.00
Summary Total 2/1/04 thru 2/29/04	Salary		8,990.00	6,733.40	8,990.00 -406.69 -440.51	-1,162.17 -557.38	-557.38 -130.36	-130.36 -71.92
Report Date Final Total 2/1/04 thru 2/29/04	Salary		8,990.00	6,733.40	8,990.00 -406.69 -440.51	-1,162.17 -557.38	-557.38 -130.36	-130.36 -71.92

Pete's Market-Student Name
Payroll Register
For the Period From Feb 1, 2004 to Feb 29, 2004
Filter Criteria includes: Report order is by Check Date. Report is printed in Detail Format.

Be sure to **enter the journal entry for $6,733.40** to transfer funds into the Payroll Checking account number 1020 from the cash account number 1010 before printing the next two reports.

b. General Journal -(check figure = $9,063.77)

Pete's Market-Student Name
General Journal
For the Period From Feb 1, 2004 to Feb 29, 2004
Filter Criteria includes: Report order is by Date. Report is printed with Accounts having Zero Amounts and with Truncated Transaction Descriptions and in Detail Format.

Date	Account ID	Reference	Trans Description	Debit Amt	Credit Amt
2/13/04	2310	MEMO	Pay 941 taxes	1,029.87	
	2330		Pay 941 taxes	1,054.00	
	2335		Pay 941 taxes	246.50	
	1010		Pay 941 taxes		2,330.37
2/29/04	1020	MEMO	Transfer net pay	6,733.40	
	1010		Transfer net pay		6,733.40
			Total	9,063.77	9,063.77

c. Trial Balance -(check figure = $84,857.49)

Filter Criteria includes: Report order is by ID. Report is printed in Detail Format.

Account ID	Account Description	Debit Amt	Credit Amt
1010	Cash	65,032.57	
2310	FIT Payable		1,162.17
2320	SIT Payable		1,322.91
2330	Social Security Tax Payable		1,114.76
2335	Medicare Tax Payable		260.72
2340	FUTA Payable		139.92
2350	SUTA Payable		857.01
3569	Pete Reel, Capital		80,000.00
5400	Wages Expense	17,490.00	
5410	Social Security Tax Expense	1,084.38	
5420	Medicare Tax Expense	253.61	
5430	FUTA Expense	139.92	
5440	SUTA Expense	857.01	
	Total:	84,857.49	84,857.49

Make a February Backup Copy

21. Click on the Company Window **File** menu; select **Backup**, include the company name and add "EndFeb" to make sure you can recognize what the backup represents. Click on **Ok**.

Advance Dates

22. We must now advance the period to prepare Peachtree for the March transactions.

♦ Using your mouse, click on **System** from the **Tasks** menu. Select **Change Accounting Periods**.

♦ Using the pull down menu, select period 3 - Mar 1, 2004 to Mar 31, 2004 and click on "**Ok**"

♦ You will be asked whether you wish to print reports before continuing. Since we have already printed our reports, we can answer "No".

♦ Note that the status bar at the bottom of the screen now reflects that you are in period 3.

Record Payment of February Payroll Liabilities and

23. Record the following general journal entry:

> 2004
> Mar. 14 Record the compound journal entry for the deposit of Social Security, Medicare, and FIT from last month's payroll.

Record March Payroll

24. Record the March payroll journal entries (be sure to dated both the payroll and the checks March 31st 2004) for Fred Flynn, Mary Jones, and Lilly Vron. Note that all three will receive other than their normal salary for this pay period.

Print Reports

25. Print the following reports accepting all defaults:

a. Payroll Register -(check figure Net = $6,439.16)

Filter Criteria includes: Report order is by Check Date. Report is printed in Detail Format.

Employee ID Employee SS No Reference Date	Pay Type	Pay Hrs	Pay Amt	Amount	Gross State SUI_ER	Fed_Income Soc_Sec_ER SDI_ER	Soc_Sec Medicare_ER	Medicare FUTA_ER
Flynn Fred Flynn 007 3/31/04	Salary		2,500.00	1,864.29	2,500.00 -123.67 -122.50	-320.79 -155.00	-155.00 -36.25	-36.25 -15.28
Jones Mary Jones 008 3/31/04	Salary		3,000.00	2,323.39	3,000.00 -126.32 -147.00	-320.79 -186.00	-186.00 -43.50	-43.50 -4.80
Vron Lilly Vron 009 3/31/04	Salary		3,000.00	2,251.48	3,000.00 -130.73 -147.00	-388.29 -186.00	-186.00 -43.50	-43.50 -8.00
Summary Total 3/1/04 thru 3/31/04	Salary		8,500.00	6,439.16	8,500.00 -380.72 -416.50	-1,029.87 -527.00	-527.00 -123.25	-123.25 -28.08
Report Date Final Total 3/1/04 thru 3/31/04	Salary		8,500.00	6,439.16	8,500.00 -380.72 -416.50	-1,029.87 -527.00	-527.00 -123.25	-123.25 -28.08

Be sure to **enter the journal entry for $6,439.16** to transfer funds into the Payroll Checking account number 1020 from the cash account number 1010 before printing the next two reports

b. General Journal -(check figure = $8,976.81)

Filter Criteria includes: Report order is by Date. Report is printed with Accounts having Zero Amounts and with Truncated Transaction Descriptions and in Detail F

Date	Account ID	Reference	Trans Description	Debit Amt	Credit Amt
3/14/04	2310	MEMO	Pay 941 taxes	1,162.17	
	2330		Pay 941 taxes	1,114.76	
	2335		Pay 941 taxes	260.72	
	1010		Pay 941 taxes		2,537.65
3/31/04	1020	MEMO	Transfer net pay	6,439.16	
	1010		Transfer net pay		6,439.16
		Total		8,976.81	8,976.81

c. Trial Balance -(check figure = $84,475.51)

Filter Criteria includes: Report order is by ID. Report is printed in Detail Format.

Account ID	Account Description	Debit Amt	Credit Amt
1010	Cash	56,055.76	
2310	FIT Payable		1,029.87
2320	SIT Payable		1,703.63
2330	Social Security Tax Payable		1,054.00
2335	Medicare Tax Payable		246.50
2340	FUTA Payable		168.00
2350	SUTA Payable		1,273.51
3569	Pete Reel, Capital		80,000.00
5400	Wages Expense	25,990.00	
5410	Social Security Tax Expense	1,611.38	
5420	Medicare Tax Expense	376.86	
5430	FUTA Expense	168.00	
5440	SUTA Expense	1,273.51	
	Total:	85,475.51	85,475.51

26. From the **Reports** menu, select **Payroll**. This will bring up a Select a Report dialogue box containing a list of several payroll reports available to us. Select the **941** folder near the bottom to open up our 941 options. Peachtree is set up to print directly on the actual government 941 form. It can also print a 941 Worksheet, which can be used to manually fill out Form 941. It will print both pages needed for a semi-weekly depositor (941 and 941B). If you have access to the blank 941 forms, you may print the report directly on the form. If not, you can still print the report on plain paper. With the **941** folder open, select **Form 941 Worksheet - 2004**. Accept all defaults by clicking on **Ok**. (check figure Block 17d = $7,198.39)

27. Close the Select a Report Window when you are finished.

28. Click on the Company Window **File** menu; select **Backup**, include the company name and add "EndMar" to make sure you can recognize what the backup represents. Click on **Ok**.

29. We must now advance the period to prepare Peachtree for the April transactions.

   ♦ Using your mouse, click on **System** from the **Tasks** menu. Select **Change Accounting Periods**.

   ♦ Using the pull down menu, select period 4 - Apr 1, 2004 to Apr 30, 2004 and click on "**Ok**"

   ♦ You will be asked whether you wish to print reports before continuing. Since we have already printed our reports, we can answer "No".

   ♦ Note that the status bar at the bottom of the screen now reflects that you are in period 4.

30. Record the following general journal entries using the **dates** listed and **reference** as "Memo":

   2004
   Apr.   15   Record the compound journal entry for the deposit of Social Security, Medicare, and FIT from last month's payroll. The total amount of the Cash account 1010 credit should be $2,330.37.
           30   Record the payment of SUTA from last quarter.
           30   Record the payment of FUTA tax owed.

31. Print the following reports accepting all defaults:

   a. General Journal -(check figure = $3,771.88)

Pete's Market-Student Name
General Journal
For the Period From Apr 1, 2004 to Apr 30, 2004
Filter Criteria includes: Report order is by Date. Report is printed with Accounts having Zero Amounts and with Truncated Transaction Descriptions and in Detail Format.

Date	Account ID	Reference	Trans Description	Debit Amt	Credit Amt
4/15/04	2310	Memo	Pay 941 taxes	1,029.87	
	2330		Pay 941 taxes	1,054.00	
	2335		Pay 941 taxes	246.50	
	1010		Pay 941 taxes		2,330.37
4/30/04	2350	Memo1	Pay SUTA taxes	1,273.51	
	1010		Pay SUTA taxes		1,273.51
4/30/04	2340	Memo2	Pay FUTA (940) taxes	168.00	
	1010		Pay FUTA (940) taxes		168.00
		Total		3,771.88	3,771.88

b. Trial Balance - (check figure = $81,703.63)

```
                                                              Pete's Market-Student Name
                                                              General Ledger Trial Balance
                                                                   As of Apr 30, 2004
Filter Criteria includes: Report order is by ID. Report is printed in Detail Format.

Account ID    Account Description              Debit Amt      Credit Amt

1010          Cash                             52,283.88
2320          SIT Payable                                      1,703.63
3569          Pete Rael, Capital                              80,000.00
5400          Wages Expense                    25,990.00
5410          Social Security Tax Expense       1,611.38
5420          Medicare Tax Expense                376.86
5430          FUTA Expense                        168.00
5440          SUTA Expense                      1,273.51

              Total:                           81,703.63      81,703.63
```

Make an April Backup Copy

32. Click on the Company Window **File** menu; select **Backup**, include the company name and add "EndApril" to make sure you can recognize what the backup represents. Click on **Ok**.

CHAPTER 6

PART A Recording Transactions in the Sales, Receipts, Purchases, and Payments Journals in The Mars Company

PART B Abby's Toy House - Mini Practice Set

Before starting on this assignment, read and complete the tasks discussed in Chapter 1 and 2

PART A: Recording Transactions in the Sales, Receipts, Purchases, and Payments Journals

Where to Record Sales and Cash Receipts

The Sales/Invoicing and Receipts features in Peachtree Complete Accounting 2005 were designed to work with the accounts receivables and general ledger modules in an integrated fashion. When transactions are recorded in the Sales/Invoicing and Receipts windows, the program automatically posts to the customer's account in the accounts receivable subsidiary ledger, records the journal entry, and posts all accounts affected in the general ledger. However, the type of transactions recorded in the Sales/Invoicing and Receipts windows in Peachtree Complete Accounting 2005 differ from the types of transactions recorded in these journals in a manual accounting system. An explanation of the differences appears in the following chart:

Name of Computerized Entry Window	Types of Transactions Recorded in Computerized Journal
Sales/Invoicing	Sales of merchandise on account Sales returns and allowances
Receipts	Cash sales and payments from credit customers on account

Computerized Aged Receivables

An Aged Receivables report (the computerized version of a schedule of accounts receivable) for The Mars Company appears below (terms of 2/10, n/30 are offered to all credit customers of The Mars Company):

The Mars Company: Customer Aged Detail As of 3/1/04

			Current	31-60	61-90	90+	Total
John Dunbar							
909	2/25/04	Invoice	500.00		--	--	500.00
Kevin Tucker							
911	2/26/04	Invoice	550.00		--	--	550.00
			1,050.00				1,050.00

Where to Record Purchases and Cash Payments

The Purchases and Payments windows in Peachtree Complete Accounting 2005 are designed to work with the accounts payable and general ledger modules in an integrated fashion.

- 50 -

When transactions are recorded in the Purchases and Payments windows, the program automatically posts to the vendor's account in the accounts payable subsidiary ledger, records the journal entry, and posts all accounts affected in the general ledger. However, the type of transactions recorded in the Purchases and Payments windows in Peachtree Complete Accounting 2005 differ from the types of transactions recorded in these journals in a manual accounting system. An explanation of the differences appears in the following chart:

Name of Computerized Journal	Types of Transactions Recorded in Computerized Journal
Purchases Window	Purchases of merchandise and other items on account
	Purchase returns and allowances
Payments Journal	Cash payments to credit and cash vendors

Aged Payables   An Aged Payables report (the computerized version of a schedule of accounts payable) for The Mars Company appears below:

The Mars Company: Vendor Aged Detail As at 3/1/04

			Current	31-60	61-90	90+	Total
Lara's Space Prints							
567	2/27/04	Invoice	435.00	--	--	--	435.00
Young's Space Simulations							
789	2/25/04	Invoice	112.00	--	--	--	112.00
			547.00	--			547.00

Open the Company Data Files

1. Double click on the Peachtree Complete 2005 icon on your desktop.

2. Open the existing company file for **The Mars Company**.

   You should back up your work before starting each chapter following instructions in Chapter 1.

Add Your Name to the company Name

3. Click on the **Maintain** menu option. Then select **Company Information**. In the **Company Name** entry field at the end of **The Mars Company**, add a dash and your name **"-Student Name"**. Click on the OK button to return to the Menu Window.

How to Record a Sale on Account

4. On March 1, 2004 sold merchandise to Kevin Tucker on account, $800, invoice #913, terms 2/10, n/30 consisting of the following:

Stock #	Description	Quantity
001	Space Age Lamp	2
002	Solar Clock	5
005	Space Shuttle Model	1

5. Select **Sales/Invoicing** from the **Tasks** menu. Using the magnifying glass next to the **Customer ID** field, select Kevin Tucker by double clicking on his name. Press the TAB key until you get to the **Date** field.   It should

already reflect Mar 1, 2004 but if not, type in the date or use the calendar to the right of the field to select the date. You are then moved to the **Invoice #** field. Type in "913". TAB until you reach the **Quantity** field. Type in "2.00" and click TAB. This will move you to the **Item** field. Using the look up menu, select the first item 001 Space Age Lamp by double clicking on it. This moves you to the **Description** field that will automatically fill in with information stored in the Inventory module. In fact, Peachtree will fill in all of the remaining fields as you tab through them until you are back to the **Quantity** field. Enter the remaining items from the above table in the same manner as the Lamp. Your screen should look like this:

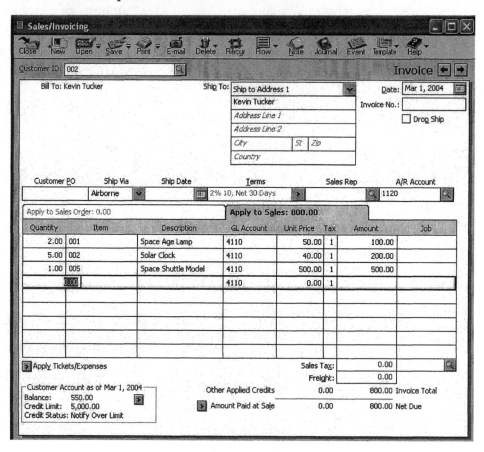

How to Review a Sales Journal

6. Before posting this transaction, you may wish to see how Peachtree will record the transaction. Click on the **Journal** icon on the tool bar. This activates a feature of Peachtree called "Accounting Behind the Screens" and allows the user a look at the workings of the program. It will bring up a Sales Journal showing exactly how it will post this invoice. That is to say, it will show you what accounts will be debited and which accounts credited. Note that Peachtree uses a perpetual inventory system and has created the entries to move the goods sold out of the Inventory account and into the Cost of Sales (COGS) account. Which will show "To be calculated".

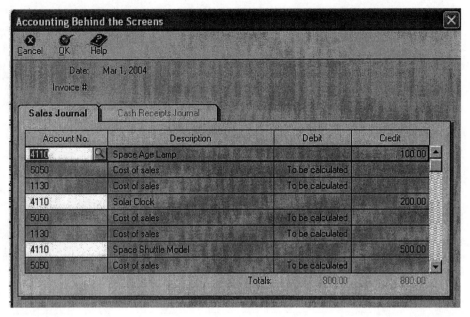

Edit a Sale or Purchase Entry Prior to Posting

7. Close the Accounting behind the screens window. If you have made an error anywhere on the invoice, simply click in the field containing the error and correct it.

How to Print/Post a Sales Entry

8. After verifying that the invoice is correct, click on the **Print** icon to print this invoice. The form default should be **Invoice Plain**. If it is not select the Change Form button and scroll until you reach Invoice Plain and select it and click OK. Select **Print**. Peachtree will print and post the transaction in one step. A blank invoice is displayed, ready for additional transactions to be recorded. If you wish to batch print later, you can simply hit the **Save** icon which will store the invoice for printing using the **Select a Report** option under the **Accounts Receivable** reports. We will print all our invoices as we create them.

How to Record a Credit Memo

9. On March 5, 2004 issued credit memorandum #CM14 to Kevin Tucker for the return of one of the lamps he purchased. Peachtree uses the same entry window, **Sales/Invoicing**, to record credits issued to customers. There are two primary differences. One is that quantities will be entered as negative amounts and the second is that the printing will be accomplished with a Credit form rather than an Invoice form.

10. Select **Sales/Invoicing** from the **Tasks** menu. Using the magnifying glass next to the **Customer ID** field, select Kevin Tucker by double clicking on his name. Press the TAB key that then moves you to the **Date** field. Type in the date "Mar 5, 2004" or use the calendar to the right of the field to select this date. You are then moved to the **Invoice #** field. Type in "CM14". TAB until you reach the **Quantity** field. Type in "-1.00" (negative one) and click TAB. This will move you to the **Item** field. Using the look up menu, select the first item 001 Space Age Lamp by double clicking on it. This moves you to the **Description** field, which will automatically fill in with information stored in the Inventory module. In fact, Peachtree will fill in all of the remaining fields as you tab through them until you are back to the **Quantity** field. Your screen should look like this:

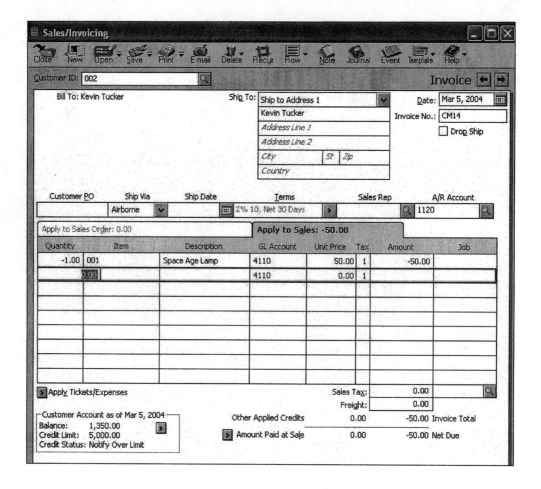

Review the Entry

11. You may again use the **Journal** icon to see what this entry will look like in the Sales Journal.

12. Close the Accounting behind the screens window. Make any corrections that may be required.

Print the Credit Memo

13. After verifying that the journal entry is correct, click on the Print icon to print this transaction. Upon clicking the Print icon, you will be brought to the **Print Forms: Invoices/Credit Memo** box. Since the last form used was the Invoice Plain, the system has defaulted to this. We require the **Negative Invoice Plain** as the form on which to print the credit memo. To be presented with a list to choose from, we must click the Change Form button **Select from all existing forms:** You are presented with a list that includes the **Negative Invoice Plain** (see the illustration at the top of the next page). Select it and printing the credit memo. If you alternate between invoices and credit memos, this process must be repeated each time the form must be changed. When you are finished, close the **Sales/Invoicing** box.

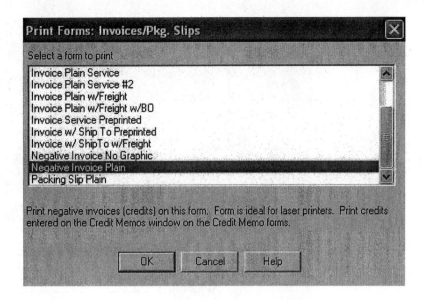

Print Forms: Invoices/Pkg. Slips ☒

Select a form to print

Invoice Plain Service
Invoice Plain Service #2
Invoice Plain w/Freight
Invoice Plain w/Freight w/BO
Invoice Service Preprinted
Invoice w/ Ship To Preprinted
Invoice w/ ShipTo w/Freight
Negative Invoice No Graphic
Negative Invoice Plain
Packing Slip Plain

Print negative invoices (credits) on this form. Form is ideal for laser printers. Print credits entered on the Credit Memos window on the Credit Memo forms.

[OK]   [Cancel]   [Help]

How to Record a Cash Receipt from a Credit Customer

14. On March 6, 2004 received check #1623 from Kevin Tucker in the amount of $550 in payment of invoice #912. Select **Receipts** from the **Tasks** menu. Peachtree will place the current date in the **Deposit ticket ID** field. Change it to the date of the transaction (030604). Using the magnifying glass, select customer Kevin Tucker. This will bring up a listing of the invoices and credits currently open in his account. The cursor will automatically move to the **Reference** field. We can enter Kevin's check number, 1623 in this field. Peachtree requires the use of a **Receipt Number** for its cash receipts. A receipt number can be assigned in the printing process. Once a numbering sequence has been started, Peachtree will automatically assign the next number. Leave the **Receipt Number** blank. Change the date to March 6, 2004. We can now select the invoice that is included in Kevin's payment. In the column marked **Pay** are small boxes that can be checked by clicking on them with the mouse. This marks the invoice selected for payment with the check received. We will check the box at the end of the line containing invoice #912. Note that the field for **Receipt Amount** automatically reflects the amount of his payment. Please note that if we were receiving cash as the result of a cash sale or for any other reason rather than a payment on account, we would use the **Apply to Revenues** tab instead of the **Apply to Invoices** tab. In that screen, we can use any GL account we like to offset the receipt of the cash. If you recorded this payment on account correctly, your screen should look like this:

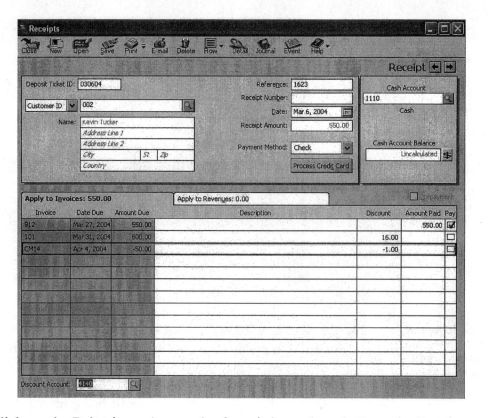

Click on the **Print** icon. Accept the form it has selected. Type the Receipt Number "101". Click **Print.**

How to Record a Subsequent Cash Receipt

15. On March 10, 2004 received check #1634 from Kevin Tucker in the amount of $735 in payment of invoice #9130 ($800), dated March 1, less credit memorandum #CM14 ($50), less 2 percent discount ($16 - 1 = $15 net sales discount). Follow the procedures above to record this receipt. Remember to check both the invoice and the credit memo. To illustrate how Peachtree can assign the Receipt Number, leave this field blank. If you recorded this payment on account correctly, your screen should look like this:

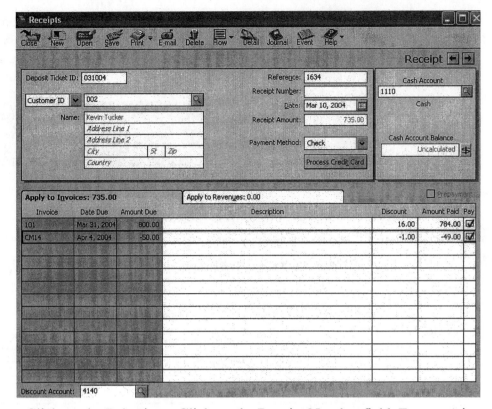

Click on the **Print** icon. Click on the Receipt Number field. Enter receipt Number "102". Click **OK** to print the Receipt.

How to Review the Receipts Journal

16. As before, we can preview how Peachtree will handle this transaction behind the screens by clicking on the **Journal** icon. This will bring up a Receipts Journal reflecting the accounts that will be affected by this entry. Close the Journal after reviewing.

17. On March 15, 2004 purchased merchandise from Young's Space Simulations on account, $165.50, invoice #7960, terms 2/10, n/30 consisting of the following:

Stock #	Description	Quantity
001	Space Age Lamp	5
004	Simulated Moon Rock	9

18. Select **Purchases/Receive Inventory** from the **Tasks** menu. Using the magnifying glass next to the **Customer ID** field, select 002 Young's Space Simulations by double clicking on his name. Press the TAB key that then moves you to the **Date** field. Type in the date "Mar 15, 2004 or use the calendar to the right of the field to select this date. You are then moved to the **Invoice #** field. Type in "7960". TAB until you reach the **Quantity** field. Type in "5.00" and click TAB. This will move you to the **Item** field. Using the look up menu, select the first item 001 Space Age Lamp by double clicking on it. This moves you to the **Description** field that will automatically fill in with information stored in the Inventory module. In fact, Peachtree will fill in all of the remaining fields as you tab through them until you are back to the **Quantity** field. Should your Unit Price be different than that brought up by Peachtree, you can easily change the amount rather than tabbing through that field. If we were purchasing something besides

merchandise inventory, we would skip over the Quantity and Item fields and fill in the Description, GL Account and Amount fields based on what we purchased and its cost. If you entered our inventory purchase correctly, your screen should look like this:

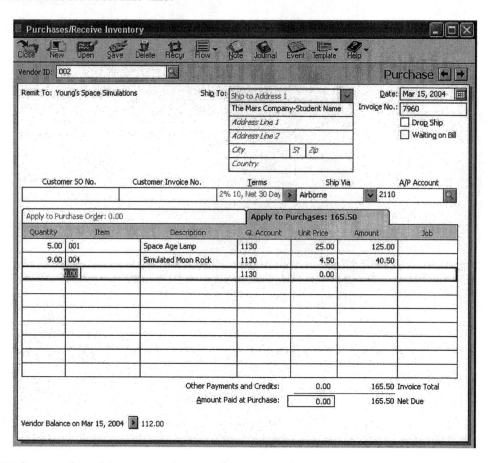

How to Review a Purchases Journal Entry

19. Before saving this transaction, you may wish to see how Peachtree will record the transaction. Click on the **Journal** icon on the tool bar. This activates a feature of Peachtree called "Accounting Behind the Screens" and allows the user a look at the workings of the program. It will bring up a Purchases Journal showing exactly how it will post this invoice. That is to say, it will show you what accounts will be debited and which accounts credited.

20. Close the Accounting Behind the Screens window. If you have made an error anywhere on the invoice, simply click in the field containing the error and correct it.

How to Post a Purchases Journal Entry

21. After verifying that the invoice is correct, click on the **Save** icon to post this transaction. A blank Purchases/Receive Inventory screen is displayed, ready for additional Purchase transactions to be recorded.

How to Record a Debit Memo

22. On March 17, 2004 returned two of the Space Age Lamps to Young's Space Simulations with a value of $50. Issued debit memo #DM27. Select **Purchases/Receive Inventory** from the **Tasks** menu. Using the magnifying glass next to the **Customer ID** field, select 002 Young's Space Simulations by double clicking on his name. Press the TAB key that then moves you to the **Date** field. Type in the date "Mar 17, 2004 or use the calendar to the right of the field to select this date. You are then moved to the **Invoice #** field. Type in "DM27". TAB until you reach the **Quantity** field. Type in "-

2.00" (negative two) and click TAB. This will move you to the **Item** field. Using the look up menu, select the first item 001 Space Age Lamp by double clicking on it. Peachtree will fill in all of the remaining fields as you tab through them until you are back to the **Quantity** field. Your screen should look like this:

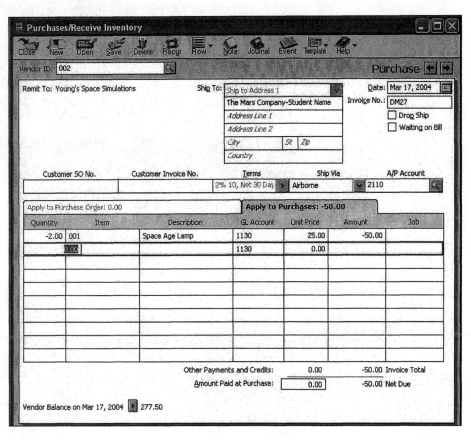

<table>
<tr><td>**How to Review a Purchases Journal Entry**</td><td>23.</td><td>Before saving this transaction, you may wish to see how Peachtree will record the transaction. Click on the **Journal** icon on the tool bar. This activates a feature of Peachtree called "Accounting Behind the Screens" and allows the user a look at the workings of the program. It will bring up a Purchases Journal showing exactly how it will post this invoice. That is to say, it will show you what accounts will be debited and which accounts credited.</td></tr>
<tr><td></td><td>24.</td><td>Close the Accounting Behind the Screens window. If you have made an error anywhere on the invoice, simply click in the field containing the error and correct it.</td></tr>
<tr><td>**Post the Entry**</td><td>25.</td><td>After verifying that the journal entry is correct, click on the **Save** icon to post this transaction; then close the Purchases window.</td></tr>
<tr><td>**How to Record a Cash Payment to a Credit Vendor**</td><td>26.</td><td>On March 25, 2004 issued check #437 to Young's Space Simulations in the amount of $225.19 in payment of invoices #790 ($112) and #7960 ($165.50), dated March 15, less debit memorandum #DM27 ($50), less 2 percent discount ($5.56 - 1.00 = $4.56 net purchases discount). Select **Payments** from the **Tasks** menu. Using the magnifying glass, select vendor Young's Space Simulations. This will bring up a listing of the invoices and credits currently open in this account. TAB to the **Date** field and type in "March 25, 2004" or use the calendar to select this date. In the column marked **Pay** are small boxes that can be checked by clicking on them with</td></tr>
</table>

the mouse. This marks the invoices selected for payment with the check you are creating. We will check the boxes at the end of the lines containing invoice #790 and #7960 and debit memo #DM27 which is associated with this invoice. If we need to make a payment for something that is not already recorded in our accounts payable, we can use the **Apply to Expenses** tab instead of the **Apply to Invoices** tab that we are using. We can write a check for any purpose, including prepaid expenses, using this feature. With our payment, note that the field for the amount of the check automatically reflects the amount of this payment. Also note that the **Check Number** field is left blank. This field is used only to enter a check that has already been written or printed. We will enter the check number when we print the check. Your screen should look like this:

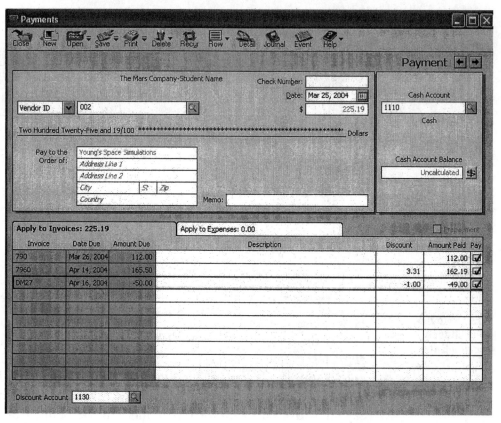

How to Review a Disbursements Journal Entry

27. Before printing this check, you may wish to see how Peachtree will record the transaction. Click on the **Journal** icon on the tool bar. It will bring up a Disbursements Journal showing exactly how it will post this payment. That is to say, it will show you what accounts will be debited and which accounts credited.

28. Close the Accounting Behind the Screens window. If you have made an error anywhere on the check, simply click in the field containing the error and correct it. If you need to change which invoice to pay, click on the red check for the incorrect invoice to deselect it and reselect the correct invoice.

How to Print a Check

29. After verifying that the check is correct, click on the **Print** icon to print this check. You will be presented with a **Print Forms: Disbursement Checks** selection box. As before, Peachtree has the ability to print on a variety of different blank check forms. Since we will be printing on plain white paper, accept the default form. You are now prompted for the check number. If Peachtree automatically fills-in a check number Highlight it and enter "437"

and select Print. The check will now print. A blank Payment window is displayed, ready for additional Payments transactions to be recorded. Close the Payments dialog box.

How to Display and Print a Customer Aged Receivables

30. From the **Reports** menu, select **Accounts Receivable**. This will bring up a Select a Report dialogue box containing a list of several receivables related reports available to us. Select **Aged Receivables** to bring up the schedule of receivables still owed to The Mars Company. Click on the **Print** icon to print the report.

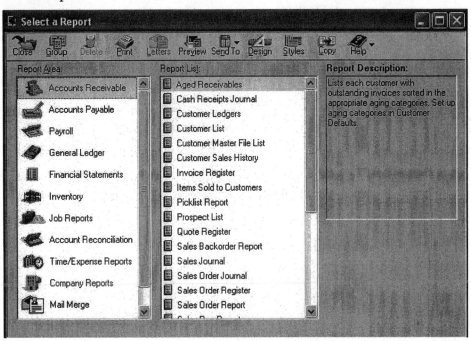

How to Display and Print a Vendor Aged Payables Report

31. Close the Aged Receivables window. From the Select a Report dialogue box, select Accounts Payable from the **Report Area** portion of the window. This will bring up a selection of payables related reports. Select **Aged Payables** to bring up the schedule of payables still owed by The Mars Company. Click on the **Print** icon to print the report.

```
                                          The Mars Company-Student Name
                                               Aged Payables
                                              As of Mar 31, 2004
Filter Criteria includes: Report order is by ID. Report is printed in Detail Format.

Vendor ID          Invoice/CM #      0 - 30     31 - 60     61 - 90   Over 90 days   Amount Due
Vendor
Contact
Telephone 1

001                569               435.00                                          435.00
Lara's Space Prints
Lara

001                                  435.00                                          435.00
Lara's Space Prints

Report Total                         435.00                                          435.00
```

Print Reports   32. Close the Aged Payables window. From the Select A Report dialogue box, select General Ledger from the **Report Area** portion of the window then print the following reports:

a.   General Ledger Trial Balance (Totals = 16,089.00)

```
                                          The Mars Company-Student Name
                                          General Ledger Trial Balance
                                               As of Mar 31, 2004
Filter Criteria includes: Report order is by ID. Report is printed in Detail Format.

Account ID   Account Description        Debit Amt     Credit Amt

1110         Cash                      11,059.81
1120         Accounts Receivable          500.00
1130         Inventory                  4,139.19
2110         Accounts Payable                            435.00
3110         Janice Mars, Capital                     14,904.00
4110         Sales                                       750.00
4140         Sales Discounts               15.00
5050         Cost of Goods Sold           375.00

             Total:                    16,089.00     16,089.00
```

b.   General Ledger Report -(Cash = $11,059.81)

The Mars Company-Student Name
General Ledger
For the Period From Mar 1, 2004 to Mar 31, 2004
Filter Criteria includes: Report order is by ID. Report is printed with Truncated Transaction Descriptions and in Detail Format.

Account ID Account Description	Date	Reference	Jrnl	Trans Description	Debit Amt	Credit Amt	Balance
1110	3/1/04			Beginning Balance			10,000.00
Cash	3/6/04	1623	CRJ	Kevin Tucker	550.00		
	3/10/04	1634	CRJ	Kevin Tucker	735.00		
	3/25/04	1007	CDJ	Young's Space Simulati		225.19	
				Current Period Change	1,285.00	225.19	1,059.81
	3/31/04			Ending Balance			11,059.81
1120	3/1/04			Beginning Balance			1,050.00
Accounts Receivable	3/1/04	101	SJ	Kevin Tucker	800.00		
	3/5/04	CM14	SJ	Kevin Tucker		50.00	
	3/6/04	1623	CRJ	Kevin Tucker - Invoic		550.00	
	3/10/04	1634	CRJ	Kevin Tucker - Invoic	50.00		
	3/10/04	1634	CRJ	Kevin Tucker - Invoic		800.00	
				Current Period Change	850.00	1,400.00	-550.00
	3/31/04			Ending Balance			500.00
1130	3/1/04			Beginning Balance			4,401.00
Inventory	3/1/04	101	COGS	Kevin Tucker - Item:		50.00	
	3/1/04	101	COGS	Kevin Tucker - Item:		250.00	
	3/1/04	101	COGS	Kevin Tucker - Item:		100.00	
	3/5/04	CM14	COGS	Kevin Tucker - Item:	25.00		
	3/15/04	7960	PJ	Young's Space Simulati	40.50		
	3/15/04	7960	PJ	Young's Space Simulati	125.00		
	3/17/04	DM27	PJ	Young's Space Simulati		50.00	
	3/25/04	1007	CDJ	Young's Space Simulati	1.00		
	3/25/04	1007	CDJ	Young's Space Simulati		3.31	
				Current Period Change	191.50	453.31	-261.81
	3/31/04			Ending Balance			4,139.19

33. You may wish to experiment with some of the other reports that are available in the various areas of Peachtree's report area. Some examples you might want to see are a Sales Journal, Purchases Journal, Cash Receipts Journal, etc. Exit the program when you are finished.

PART B: Abby's Toy House – Practice Set

Open the Company Data Files

1. Double click on the Peachtree Complete Accounting 2005 icon on your desktop.

2. Open the existing company file for **Abby's Toy House**.

3. You should back up your file before starting to work on each new company following the instructions in Chapter 1.

Add Your Name to the company Name

4. Click on the **Maintain** menu option. Then select **Company Information**. The program will respond by bringing up a dialogue box allowing the user to edit/add information about the company. In the **Company Name** entry field at the end of **Abby's Toy House**, add a dash and your name "**-Student Name**" to the end of the company name. Click on the OK button to return to the Menu Window.

Record Transactions

5. Record the following transactions using the appropriate General(G), Sales/Invoicing(S), Receipts(R), Purchases/Receive Inventory (PU), and Payments(PA) windows. Use the same forms when printing invoices, credits and checks as in Part A changing the starting numbers as needed. The transactions for March:

2004
Mar. 1 Abby Ellen invested $8,000 in the toy store. (G)

1 Paid three months' rent in advance, using an electronic funds transfer (EFT), $3,000. (G)

3 Purchased merchandise from Earl Miller Company on account, $4,000, invoice # 410, terms 2/10, n/30 consisting of the following: 6- Mountain Bikes, 12- Bike Carriers, 8- Deluxe Bike Seats. (PU)

3 Sold merchandise to Bill Burton on account, $1,000, invoice # 1, terms 2/10, n/30 consisting of the following: 1- Mountain Bike, 1- Bike Carrier. (S)

6 Sold merchandise to Jim Rex on account, $700, invoice # 2, terms 2/10, n/30 consisting of the following: 3- Bike Carriers, 1- Deluxe Bike Seat. (S)

10 Purchased merchandise from Earl Miller Co. on account $1,200, invoice # 415, terms 2/10, n/30 consisting of the following: 2- Mountain Bikes, 4- Bike Carriers. (PU)

10 Sold merchandise to Bill Burton on account, $600, invoice # 3, terms 2/10, n/30 consisting of the following: 3- Bike Carriers. (S)

10 Paid cleaning service $300, using an EFT (G)

11 Jim Rex returned merchandise that cost $300 to Abby's Toy House consisting of the following: 1- Bike Carrier, 1- Deluxe Bike Seat. Abby issued credit memorandum # 1 (CM1) to Jim Rex for $300. (S) Remember to use negative quantities and the Negative Invoice Plain form.

11 Purchased merchandise from Minnie Katz on account, $4,000, invoice # 311, terms 2/10, n/30 consisting of the following: 2- Doll Houses w/ Furniture, 4- Porcelain Face Dolls, 10- Yo Yo's, Designer, 10- Magic Kits. (PU)

12 Issued check # 1 to Earl Miller Co. in the amount of $3,920 in payment of invoice # 410 ($4,000), dated March 2, less 2 percent discount ($80). (PA)

13 Sold $1,300 of toy merchandise for cash consisting of the following: 1- Doll House w/ Furniture, 1- Magic Kit. (Use the Receipts window skip the Customer ID field. Type "CASH" in the Name and Reference fields. Use Receipt Number "1". Change Payment Method to Cash. Use the Apply to Revenues tab and list the items sold accepting all other defaults.)

13 Paid salaries, $600, using an EFT (G)

14 Returned merchandise to Minnie Katz in the amount of $1,000 consisting of the following: 1- Doll House w/ Furniture, 2-Porcelain Face Dolls. Abby's Toy House issued debit memorandum # 1. (PU) Remember to enter quantity as negative.

14 Sold merchandise for $4,000 cash consisting of the following: 3- Mountain Bikes, 3- Bike Carriers, 2- Magic Kits, 4- Yo Yo's, Designer. Use Receipt Number "2". See transaction from March 13 for procedures. (R)

16 Received check # 9823 from Jim Rex in the amount of

$392 in payment of invoice # 2 ($700), dated March 6, less credit memorandum # 1 ($300), less 2 percent discount ($14 - 6 = $8 net sales discount). Use Receipt Number "3". (R)

16   Received check # 4589 from Bill Burton in the amount of $1,000 in payment of invoice # 1, dated March 2. Use Receipt Number "4". (R) Notice how Peachtree does not factor in the discount since it is past the discount date.

16   Sold merchandise to Amy Rose on account, $4,000, invoice # 4, terms 2/10, n/30 consisting of the following: 1 Porcelain Face Doll, 3- Mountain Bikes, 4- Bike Carriers, 3 Deluxe Bike Seats. Remember to use the Invoice Plain form. (S)

21   Purchased delivery truck on account from Sam Katz Garage, $3,000, invoice # 111, terms 2% 10, n/30. (PU) Since this is not an inventory item, you do not need to fill in the **Item** field. You must type in the **Description**. Peachtree will default the GL code to a delivery truck since this vendor was set up to do so. You will need to type in the purchase price in the **Amount** field.

22   Sold to Bill Burton merchandise on account, $900, invoice # 5, terms 2/10, n/30 consisting of the following: 3- Magic Kits. (S)

23   Issued check # 2 to Minnie Katz in the amount of $2,970 in payment of invoice # 311 ($4,000), dated March 11, less debit memorandum # 1 ($1,000), less 1 percent discount ($40 - 10 = $30 net purchases discount). (PA)

24   Sold toy merchandise on account to Amy Rose, $1,100, invoice # 6, terms 2/10, n/30 consisting of the following: 1- Porcelain Face Doll, 1- Magic Kit, 3- Yo Yo's, Designer. (S). Select yes when the over credit limit message appears.

25   Purchased toy merchandise for cash from Woody Smith while waiting for an account to be approved, $600, check # 3 consisting of the following: 2- Marionettes, Hand Carved. (Use the Payments window, Apply to Expenses tab and list the items purchased)

27   Purchased toy merchandise from Woody Smith on account, $4,800, invoice # 211, terms 2/10, n/30 consisting of the following: 16- Marionettes, Hand Carved. (PU)

28   Received check # 4598 from Bill Burton in the amount of $882 in payment of invoice # 5 ($900),

dated March 22, less 2 percent discount ($18). Use Receipt Number "5". (R)

28 Received check # 3217 from Amy Rose in the amount of $1,078 in payment of invoice # 6, dated March 24, less 2 percent discounts ($22). Use Receipt Number "6". (R)

28 Abby invested an additional $5,000 in the business. (G)

29 Purchased merchandise on account from Earl Miller Co. $1,400, invoice # 436, terms 2/10, n/30 consisting of the following: 3- Mountain Bike, 2- Bike Carriers. (PU)

30 Issued check # 4 to Earl Miller Co. in the amount of $1,372 in payment of invoice # 436 ($1,400), dated March 29, less 2 percent discount ($28). (PA)

30 Sold merchandise to Bonnie Flow Company on account, $3,000, invoice # 7, terms 2/10, n/30 consisting of the following: 5- Marionettes, Hand Carved. (S)

Print Reports 5. Print the following reports accepting all defaults:

a. Aged Receivables

					Abby's Toy House	
					Aged Receivables	
					As of Mar 31, 2004	

Filter Criteria includes: Report order is by ID. Report is printed in Detail Format.

Customer ID Customer Contact Telephone 1	Invoice/CM #	0-30	31-60	61-90	Over 90 days	Amount Due
001 Amy Rose		4,000.00				4,000.00
002 Bill Burton Bill	1 3	1,000.00 600.00				1,000.00 600.00
002 Bill Burton		1,600.00				1,600.00
003 Bonnie Flow Company Bonnie	7	3,000.00				3,000.00
003 Bonnie Flow Company		3,000.00				3,000.00
Report Total		8,600.00				8,600.00

b. Aged Payables

Filter Criteria includes: Report order is by ID. Report is printed in Detail Format.

Vendor ID Vendor Contact Telephone 1	Invoice/CM #	0 - 30	31 - 60	61 - 90	Over 90 days	Amount Due
001 Earl Miller Company Earl	415	1,200.00				1,200.00
001 Earl Miller Company		1,200.00				1,200.00
003 Sam Katz Garage Sam	111	3,000.00				3,000.00
003 Sam Katz Garage		3,000.00				3,000.00
004 Woody Smith Woody	211	4,800.00				4,800.00
004 Woody Smith		4,800.00				4,800.00

c. General Journal

Filter Criteria includes: Report order is by Date. Report is printed with Accounts having Zero Amounts and with Truncated Transaction Descriptions and in Detail Fo

Date	Account ID	Reference	Trans Description	Debit Amt	Credit Amt
3/1/04	1140	EFT	Prepaid 3 months rent	3,000.00	
	1110		Prepaid 3 months rent		3,000.00
3/1/04	1110	Memo	Owner investment	8,000.00	
	3110		Owner investment		8,000.00
3/10/04	5620	EFT	Cleaning service payment	300.00	
	1110		Cleaning service payment		300.00
3/13/04	5610	EFT	Paid salaries	600.00	
	1110		Paid salaries		600.00
3/28/04	1110	Invest	Owner Investment	5,000.00	
	3110		Owner Investment		5,000.00
		Total		16,900.00	16,900.00

d. General Ledger Report

Filter Criteria includes: Report order is by ID. Report is printed with Truncated Transaction Descriptions and in Detail Format.

Account ID Account Description	Date	Reference	Jrnl	Trans Description	Debit Amt	Credit Amt	Balance
1110	3/1/04			Beginning Balance			
Cash	3/1/04	Memo	GENJ	Owner investment	8,000.00		
	3/1/04	EFT	GENJ	Prepaid 3 months rent		3,000.00	
	3/1/04	2	CDJ	Minnie Katz		2,970.00	
	3/10/04	EFT	GENJ	Cleaning service paym		300.00	
	3/12/04	1	CDJ	Earl Miller Company		3,920.00	
	3/13/04	Cash	CRJ		1,300.00		
	3/13/04	EFT	GENJ	Paid salaries		600.00	
	3/14/04	Cash	CRJ		4,000.00		
	3/16/04	9823	CRJ	Jim Rex	392.00		
	3/25/04	3	CDJ	Woody Smith		600.00	
	3/28/04	4598	CRJ	Bill Burton	882.00		
	3/28/04	3217	CRJ	Amy Rose	1,078.00		
	3/28/04	Invest	GENJ	Owner Investment	5,000.00		
	3/30/04	4	CDJ	Earl Miller Company		1,372.00	
				Current Period Change	20,652.00	12,762.00	7,890.00
	3/31/04			Ending Balance			7,890.00
1120	3/1/04			Beginning Balance			
Accounts Receivable	3/3/04	1	SJ	Bill Burton	1,000.00		
	3/6/04	2	SJ	Jim Rex	700.00		
	3/10/04	3	SJ	Bill Burton	600.00		
	3/11/04	CM1	SJ	Jim Rex		300.00	
	3/16/04	9823	CRJ	Jim Rex - Invoice: 2		700.00	
	3/16/04	9823	CRJ	Jim Rex - Invoice: CM	300.00		
	3/16/04	4	SJ	Amy Rose	4,000.00		
	3/22/04	5	SJ	Bill Burton	900.00		
	3/24/04	6	SJ	Amy Rose	1,100.00		
	3/28/04	4598	CRJ	Bill Burton - Invoice:		900.00	

e.   General Ledger Trial Balance

Filter Criteria includes: Report order is by ID. Report is printed in Detail Format.

Account ID	Account Description	Debit Amt	Credit Amt
1110	Cash	7,890.00	
1120	Accounts Receivable	8,600.00	
1130	Inventory	6,712.00	
1140	Prepaid Rent	3,000.00	
1150	Delivery Truck	3,000.00	
2110	Accounts Payable		9,000.00
3110	Abby Ellen, Capital		13,000.00
4110	Sales		16,300.00
4140	Sales Discounts	48.00	
5050	Cost of Goods Sold	8,150.00	
5610	Salaries Expense	600.00	
5620	Cleaning Expense	300.00	
	Total:	38,300.00	38,300.00

CHAPTER 7

Accounting Cycle for a Merchandise Company – The Corner Dress Shop Mini Practice Set

Before starting on this assignment, read and complete the assignments for Chapters 1 through 6

This practice set will help you review all the key concepts of a merchandise company along with the integration of payroll, including the preparation of Form 941.

Since you are the bookkeeper on The Corner Dress Shop, we have gathered the following information for you. It will be your task to complete the accounting cycle for March.

The Corner Dress Shop: Trial Balance As at 3/1/04

		Debits	Credits
1110	Cash	2,502.90	—
1115	Petty Cash	35.00	—
1120	Accounts Receivable	2,200.00	—
1130	Inventory	5,600.00	—
1140	Prepaid Rent	1,800.00	—
1250	Delivery Truck	6,000.00	—
1251	Accum. Dep—Delivery Truck	—	1,500.00
2110	Accounts Payable	—	1,900.00
2310	Federal Income Tax Payable	—	1,284.00
2320	State Income Tax Payable	—	756.00
2330	FICA- Soc. Sec. Payable	—	1,339.20
2335	FICA- Medicare Payable	—	313.20
2340	FUTA Payable	—	163.20
2350	SUTA Payable	—	979.20
2400	Unearned Rent	—	800.00
3110	Betty Loeb, Capital	—	9,103.10
		18,137.90	18,137.90

The Corner Dress Shop: Customer Aged Detail As at 3/1/04

			Total	Current	31 to 60	61 to 90
Bing Co.						
12	1/1/04	Invoice	2,200.00	—	2,200.00	—

The Corner Dress Shop: Vendor Aged Detail As at 3/1/04

Blew Co.

			Total	Current	31 to 60	61 to 90
422	2/15/04	Invoice	1,900.00	1,900.00	—	—

The Corner Dress Shop, owned by Betty Loeb, is located at 1 Milgate Road, Marblehead, Massachusetts, 01945. Her employer identification number is 33-4158215. Federal Income Tax (FIT), State Income Tax (SIT), Social Security, Medicare, FUTA, and SUTA are all calculated automatically by the program based on the following assumptions and built-in tax rates:

♦ FICA: Social Security, 6.2 percent on $80,400; Medicare, 1.45 percent on all earnings (we are using parameters for the year 2001).

♦ SUTA: 3.2 percent on the first $7,000 in earnings.

♦ CASDI: 0.9 percent on the first $46,327 in earnings.

♦ FUTA: 0.8 percent on the first $7,000 in earnings.

♦ Employees are paid monthly. The payroll is recorded and paid on the last day of each month.

♦ FIT is calculated automatically by the program based on the marital status and number of exemptions claimed by each employee. These have been set up already. The tables will accommodate only single and married as they currently exist. In a full version of the program, all statuses would be available. In addition, with the full version of the program, the user would subscribe to Peachtree's Tax Table Service, which would periodically update the tax tables to insure accuracy in the calculations. Since the 2004 tax data is not available, the numbers calculated in this book are not accurate.

♦ SIT for California is calculated automatically by the program based on the marital status and number of exemptions claimed by each employee. FICA: Social Security, 6.2 percent on $76,200; Medicare, 1.45 percent on all earnings.

Open the Company Data Files

1. Double click on the Peachtree Complete 2005 icon to open the program.

2. Open the existing company file for **The Corner Dress Shop**.

You should back up your work before starting each chapter following instructions in Chapter 1.

Add Your Name to the company Name

3. Click on the **Maintain** menu option. Then select **Company Information**. The program will respond by bringing up a dialogue box allowing the user to edit/add information about the company. In the **Company Name** entry field at the end of **The Corner Dress Shop**, add a dash and your name "-**Student Name**" to the end of the company name. Click on the OK button to return to the Menu Window.

Printing an Inventory Valuation Report

4. To see what inventory items The Corner Dress Shop has available, let's print a listing. Select **Inventory** from the **Reports** menu. Select Inventory Valuation Report from the Reports List. Accept all defaults and print the resulting report. You will see that we have 6 items in our inventory. In addition, we can see our current cost on each item. Save this report to compare with a similar report you will print at the end of this practice set.

5.   Peachtree's Inventory module allows the user to easily add new items or make changes to existing items such as recording price changes. Since you will be asked to change prices later in the practice set, let's take a look at how that works now. Do not actually change any of the fields for the item we will be looking at.

♦   Select **Inventory Items** from the **Maintain** menu.

♦   In the **Item ID** field, select "6000" using the Look Up feature.

♦   In the **Description** field, you will see the current description of this inventory item. Should a change be needed, we would simply place the cursor where the change needs to be made and edit as needed.

♦   Under the **General** Tab is a field where we can select and then enter a longer description of this item that will appear on sales and/or purchase invoices when we include this item on sales or purchase invoices.

♦   The current selling price for this item is kept in the **Price Level 1** field. Peachtree has the capability of storing multiple prices for an item. This feature can be activated by clicking on the arrow to the right of the **Price Level 1** field. Go ahead and click on this arrow. A table is presented which allows us to enter up to 10 different selling prices. Different customers can be assigned to different price levels in this manner. Since we have only one price, we can **Cancel** the Multiple Price Levels box to return to the Maintain Inventory Items window. When you are prompted to change prices later in the practice set, you will simply change the price in the **Price Level 1** field rather than add multiple prices.

♦   Unit/Measure, Item Type and Location are sorting and information fields that can be used as needed and have no restrictions as to content except length.

♦   The **Cost Method** field is where we can select the cost assumption to use with this item. When initially entering the item, you can use the pull down menu, to see that our selection consists of FIFO, LIFO or Average. Once saved, the cost method cannot be changed.

♦   Peachtree has used default information to select the GL accounts needed for an inventory transaction. If there is some need to change these, we can decline the defaults and select any account we may need. Since there is no need to change these accounts, we will leave them at their default settings.

♦   We could also establish a minimum stock level and have Peachtree warn us when we fall below this level. We can also establish a reorder point that Peachtree can use to generate an inventory reorder listing.

♦   We can also select the vendor from whom we would normally order this item. Peachtree uses this and all the information we can see in this window to work interactively with Peachtree's other modules and report features.

♦   Your screen should look like this:

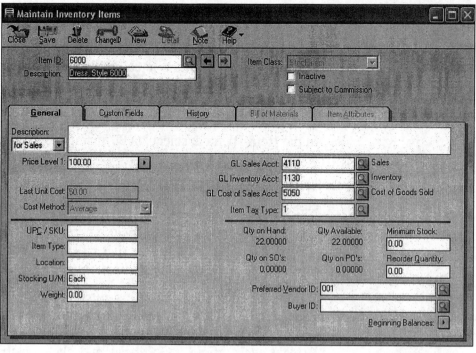

**Record March
Transactions**

6. Record the following transactions using the appropriate General (G), Sales/Invoicing (S), Receipts(R), Purchases/Receive Inventory (PU), and Payments (PA) windows. Use the same forms when printing invoices, credits and checks as in Chapter 6 changing the starting numbers as needed. If prompted for a Cash account, select **Cash**. Accept defaults for any field for which you are not given data. Use the date of the transaction for the Deposit Ticket ID field. The transactions for March:

2004

Mar. 1 Received check no. 7634 from the Bing Co. in the amount of $2,200 in payment of invoice no. 12 ($2,200), dated January 1. Receipt No. 101 (R)

3 Purchased merchandise from the Morris Co. on account, $10,000, invoice no. 1210, terms 2/10, n/30 consisting of 184- Style 1000 and 180- Style 2000 dresses. (P)

3 Sold merchandise to the Ronold Co. on account, $7,000, invoice no. 51, terms 2/10, n/30 consisting of 48- Style 1000, 30- Style 2000, 8- Style 3000, 9- Style 4000, 8- Style 5000 and 8- Style 6000 dresses. (S)

7 Sold merchandise to the Ronold Co. on account, $5,000, invoice no. 52, terms 2/10, n/30 consisting of 48- Style 1000, 24- Style 2000, 5- Style 3000, 3- Style 4000, 3- Style 5000 and 3- Style 6000 dresses. (S)

10 Purchased merchandise from the Morris Co. on account, $5,000, invoice no. 1286, terms 2/10, n/30 consisting of 92- Style 1000 and 90- Style 2000 dresses. (P)

10 Sold merchandise to the Ronold Co. on account $3,000, invoice no. 53, terms 2/10, n/30 consisting of 20- Style 1000, 20- Style 2000, 4- Style 3000, 2- Style

4000 and 4- Style 5000 dresses. (S)

10 Paid cleaning service $300, check no. 110 to Ronda's Cleaning Service. In the Payments window:

- ♦ Skip the Vendor ID field

- ♦ Enter Ronda's name in the Name field
- ♦ Enter a short description in the description field on the apply to expenses tab
- ♦ Select the correct GL account for this line (Cleaning Expense-5510)
- ♦ Enter the amount in the Amount column.
- ♦ Print the check as you did in Chapter 6. (PA)

11 Ronold Co. returned merchandise that cost $1,000 from invoice no. 52 consisting of 4- Style 1000, 5- Style 2000, 2- Style 3000, 1- Style 4000, 2- Style 5000 and 1- Style 6000 dresses. The Corner Dress Shop issued credit memorandum no. CM 10 to the Ronald Co. for $1,000. Remember to use negative quantities and the Negative Invoice Plain form for returns. (S)

11 Purchased merchandise from the Jones Co. on account $10,000, invoice no. 4639, terms 1/15, n/60 consisting of 144- Style 3000 and 124- Style 4000 dresses. (P)

12 Issued check no. 111 to the Morris Co. in the amount of $9,800 in payment of invoice no. 1210 ($10,000), dated March 2, less 2 percent discount ($200). (PA)

13 Sold $7,000 of merchandise for cash consisting of 24- Style 1000, 30- Style 2000, 24- Style 3000 and 29- Style 4000 dresses. Skip the Customer ID field and type "CASH" in the name filed and the Reference field. Receipt No. 102. (R)

14 Returned merchandise to the Jones Co. in the amount of $2,000 consisting of 32- Style 3000 and 22- Style 4000 dresses. Remember to use negative quantities for returns. Assign DM 4 as the invoice number. (P)

15 Print a Trial Balance first to determine how much to pay for each account and pay FIT, Social Security, and Medicare taxes due for February payroll, check no. 112 in the amount of $2,936.40. Skip the vendor ID field and type "IRS" in the name field. Be sure to put the correct GL Code for each payable account. (PA)

15 Due to increased operating costs, The Corner Dress Shop must raise its selling prices as follows:

Style 1000	$60.00
Style 2000	$70.00
Style 3000	$80.00
Style 4000	$90.00
Style 5000	$110.00
Style 6000	$120.00

Make these changes using the procedures discussed at the start of this practice set before continuing.

15 Sold merchandise for $29,000 cash consisting of 124- Style 1000, 144- Style 2000, 72- Style 3000, 61- Style 4000, 1- Style 5000 and 1- Style 6000 dresses. Skip the Customer ID field. Type "CASH" in the Name and Reference fields. Receipt No. 103. If you do not end up with $29,000 as your total, check to make sure you accomplished the price changes correctly. (R) If you get the message that the reference number has already been entered for this customer click OK to continue.

15 Betty Loeb withdrew $100 for her own personal expenses, check no. 113. (PA) Skip the Vendor ID and enter her name in the name field. Be sure to code to Owners Withdrawals (3120)

15 Paid SIT tax for February payroll, check no. 114. Skip the Vendor ID field. Make the check payable to the State of Massachusetts (using the name field). The check should be in the amount of $756.00. (PA)

17 Received check no. 5432 from the Ronold Co. in the amount of $3,920 in payment of invoice no. 52 ($5,000), dated March 7, less credit memo CM 10 ($1,000), less 2 percent discount ($100 - 20 = $80, net sales discount). Receipt No. 104. (R)

17 Received check no. 5447 from the Ronold Co. in the amount of $7,000 in payment of invoice no. 51, dated March 3. Receipt No. 105. (R)

17 Sold merchandise to the Bing Co. on account, $3,200, invoice no. 54, terms 2/10, n/30 consisting of 12- Style 1000, 10- Style 2000, 11- Style 3000 and 10- Style 4000 dresses. Be sure to change the invoice form when printing. (S)

21 Purchased delivery truck on account from Moe's Garage, invoice no. 7113, $17,200. (PU)

- Select Moe's Garage in the Vendor ID field
- Enter the date and invoice number
- Enter a description of the payment in that field
- Select the correct GL account for this line (Delivery Truck)
- Enter the amount in the Amount column.
- Save

22 Sold merchandise to the Ronold Co. on account $4,000, invoice no 55, terms 2/10, n/30 consisting of 24- Style 1000, 24- Style 2000, 3- Style 3000, 2- Style 4000, 2- Style 5000 and 2- Style 6000 dresses. (S)

23 Issued check no. 115 to the Jones Co. in the amount of $7,920 in payment of invoice no. 4639 ($10,000),

dated March 11, less debit memo no. DM 4 ($2,000), less 1 percent discount ($100 - 20 = $80 net purchases discount). (PA)

24 Sold merchandise to the Bing Co. on account, $2,000, invoice no. 56, terms 2/10 n./30 consisting of 1- Style 2000, 10- Style 3000, 10- Style 4000, 1- Style 5000 and 1- Style 6000 dresses. (S).

25 Purchased merchandise for $1,000 cash from the Jones Company, check no. 116, consisting of, 16- Style 3000 and 11- Style 4000 dresses. Skip the Vendor ID field and type "Jones Company" in the name field. Use the Quantity and Item fields in the Payments window just as you would in the Purchases window. (PA)

27 Purchased merchandise from the Blew Co. on account, $6,000, invoice no. 437, terms 2/10, n/30 consisting of, 60- Style 5000 and 66- Style 6000 dresses. (P)

28 Received check no. 5562 from the Ronold Co. in the amount of $3,920 in payment of invoice no. 55 ($4,000), dated March 22, less 2 percent discount ($80). Receipt No. 106. (R)

28 Received check no. 8127 from the Bing Co. in the amount of $3,200 in payment of invoice no. 54, dated March 16. Receipt Number 107. (R)

29 Purchased merchandise from the Morris Co. on account, $9,000, invoice no. 1347, terms 2/10, n/30 consisting of, 150- Style 1000 and 150- Style 2000 dresses. The vendor has changed his prices on these items so instead of accepting Peachtree's default for the unit prices, enter $28.00 and $32.00 for the Style 1000 and style 2000 respectively. (P)

30 Sold merchandise to the Bing Co. on account, $10,000, invoice no. 57, terms 2/10, n/30 consisting of 6- Style 3000, 5- Style 4000, 41- Style 5000 and 38- Style 6000 dresses. (S).

30 The Auxiliary Petty Cash Record for March listed the following: Postage Expense, $5; Delivery Expense, $10; Cleaning Expense, $6; Miscellaneous Expense, $10. Issued check no. 117 to replenish the petty cash fund. Skip the Vendor ID field and type "CASH" in the name field. (PA)

31 Issued payroll checks for March wages as follows:

Employee	March Wages	Check no.
Case, Mel	$3,325	118
Holl, Jane	4,120	119
Moore, Jackie	4,760	120

Use **Select for _P_ayroll Entry** under the **Tas_k_s** menu. Use 31 March as the Pay End date as well as for the check date. Use the Cash account number 1110 to issue the checks.

7. Print the following reports:

   a. General Ledger Trial Balance

The Corner Dress Shop
General Ledger Trial Balance
As of Mar 31, 2004

Filter Criteria includes: Report order is by ID. Report is printed in Detail Format.

Account ID	Account Description	Debit Amt	Credit Amt
1110	Cash	26,587.35	
1115	Petty Cash	35.00	
1120	Accounts Receivable	15,000.00	
1130	Inventory	13,515.00	
1135	Inventory-Purchase Discounts		280.00
1140	Prepaid Rent	1,800.00	
1250	Delivery Truck	23,200.00	
1251	Accum. Dep-Delivery Truck		1,500.00
2110	Accounts Payable		39,100.00
2310	Federal Income Tax Payable		1,382.09
2320	State Income Tax Payable		577.08
2330	FICA- Soc. Sec. Payable		1,513.42
2335	FICA- Medicare Payable		353.94
2340	FUTA Payable		260.84
2350	SUTA Payable		1,565.04
2400	Unearned Rent		800.00
3110	Betty Loeb, Capital		9,103.10
3120	Betty Loeb, Withdrawals	100.00	
4110	Sales		69,200.00
4140	Sales Discounts	160.00	
5050	Cost of Goods Sold	31,085.00	
5100	Delivery Expense	10.00	
5400	Salaries Expense	12,205.00	
5420	Payroll Tax Expense	1,617.16	
5500	Postage Expense	5.00	
5510	Cleaning Expense	306.00	
5560	Miscellaneous Expense	10.00	
	Total:	125,635.51	125,635.51

   b. Aged Receivables

The Corner Dress Shop
Aged Receivables
As of Mar 31, 2004

Filter Criteria includes: Report order is by ID. Report is printed in Detail Format.

Customer ID Customer Contact Telephone 1	Invoice/CM #	0-30	31-60	61-90	Over 90 days	Amount Due
001 Bing Company	56	2,000.00				2,000.00
	57	10,000.00				10,000.00
001 Bing Company		12,000.00				12,000.00
003 Ronold Company	53	3,000.00				3,000.00
003 Ronold Company		3,000.00				3,000.00
Report Total		15,000.00				15,000.00

   c. Aged Payables

- 76 -

The Corner Dress Shop
Aged Payables
As of Mar 31, 2004

Filter Criteria includes: Report order is by ID. Report is printed in Detail Format.

Vendor ID Vendor Contact Telephone 1	Invoice/CM #	0 - 30	31 - 60	61 - 90	Over 90 days	Amount Due
001 Blew Company		7,900.00				7,900.00
003 Moe's Garage	7113	17,200.00				17,200.00
003 Moe's Garage		17,200.00				17,200.00
004 Morris Company	1286 1347	5,000.00 9,000.00				5,000.00 9,000.00
004 Morris Company		14,000.00				14,000.00
Report Total		39,100.00				39,100.00

d. Payroll Register

The Corner Dress Shop
Payroll Register
For the Period From Mar 1, 2004 to Mar 31, 2004

Filter Criteria includes: Report order is by Check Date. Report is printed in Detail Format.

Employee ID Employee SS No Reference Date	Pay Type	Pay Hrs	Pay Amt	Amount	Gross State SUI_ER	Fed_Income Soc_Sec_ER SDI_ER	Soc_Sec Medicare_ER	Medicare FUTA_ER
001 Mel Case 118 3/31/04	Salary		3,325.00	2,633.97	3,325.00 -143.54 -159.60	-293.13 -206.15	-206.15 -48.21	-48.21 -26.60
002 Jane Holl 119 3/31/04	Salary		4,120.00	3,164.85	4,120.00 -190.09 -197.76	-449.88 -255.44	-255.44 -59.74	-59.74 -32.96
003 Jackie Moore 120 3/31/04	Salary		4,760.00	3,513.33	4,760.00 -243.45 -228.48	-639.08 -295.12	-295.12 -69.02	-69.02 -38.08
Summary Total 3/1/04 thru 3/31/04	Salary		12,205.00	9,312.15	12,205.00 -577.08 -585.84	-1,382.09 -756.71	-756.71 -176.97	-176.97 -97.64
Report Date Final Total 3/1/04 thru 3/31/04	Salary		12,205.00	9,312.15	12,205.00 -577.08 -585.84	-1,382.09 -756.71	-756.71 -176.97	-176.97 -97.64

e. Form 941 Worksheet – 2004

The Corner Dress Shop

Summary Payroll Report

Form 941 Worksheet

Quarter-To-Date for the Quarter Ending

March 31, 2004

Employer identification number   33-4158215

1. Number of employees in the pay period that includes March 12 (January-March calendar quarter return only)				
2. Total wages and tips, plus other compensation...............				12,205.00
3. Total income tax withheld from wages, tips, and sick pay				1,382.09
4. Adjustment of withheld income tax for preceding quarters of calendar year........				
5. Adjusted total of income tax withheld. (If you entered an adjustment on line 4, add line 4 to line 3. If there is no adjustment on line 4, this line is equal to line 3.)............				
6a. Taxable social security wages.......	12,205.00	x .124	6b.	1,513.42
6c. Taxable social security tips........		x .124	6d.	
7a. Taxable Medicare wages and tips.........	12,205.00	x .029	7b.	353.94
8. Total social security and Medicare taxes (add lines 6b, 6d and 7b)				
9. Adjustment of social security and Medicare taxes Sick Pay _____ +/- Fractions of Cents _____ +/- Other _____ =				
10. Adjusted total of social security and Medicare taxes. (If you entered an adjustment on line 9, add line 9 to line 8. If there is no adjustment on line 9, this line is equal to line 8.)........				
11. Total taxes (add lines 5 and 10)...........				
12. Advanced earned income credit (EIC) payments made to employees, if any				
13. Net taxes (subtract line 12 from line 11). This should equal line 17, column (d) below				
14. Total deposits for quarter, including overpayment applied from a prior quarter.......				
15. Balance Due (subtract line 14 from line 13)...........				

16. Overpayment, if line 14 is more than line 13, enter excess here. _____

17 Monthly Summary of Federal Tax Liability	(a) 1st month liability	(b) 2nd month liability	(c) 3rd month liability	(d) Total liability for Qtr
Before adjustments			3,249.45	3,249.45
Adjustments				
After adjustments				

Record March Adjusting Entries

8. Open the General Journal; date the transaction 3/31/04 and use the reference number "Adjustments" then record adjusting journal entries based on the following adjustment data:

   a. During March, rent expired, $600.

   b. Truck depreciated $150.

   c. Rental income earned, $200 (Use unearned rent for the debit account).

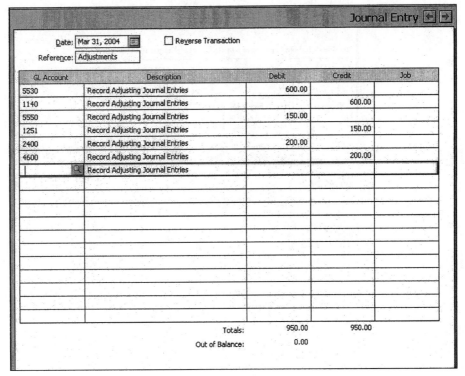

Journal Entry ← →

Date: Mar 31, 2004
Reference: Adjustments
☐ Reverse Transaction

GL Account	Description	Debit	Credit	Job
5530	Record Adjusting Journal Entries	600.00		
1140	Record Adjusting Journal Entries		600.00	
5550	Record Adjusting Journal Entries	150.00		
1251	Record Adjusting Journal Entries		150.00	
2400	Record Adjusting Journal Entries	200.00		
4600	Record Adjusting Journal Entries		200.00	
	Record Adjusting Journal Entries			

Totals: 950.00 950.00
Out of Balance: 0.00

Print Reports   9.   After you have posted the adjusting journal entries, close the General Journal; then print the following reports:

a.   General Journal

The Corner Dress Shop
General Journal
For the Period From Mar 1, 2004 to Mar 31, 2004
Filter Criteria includes: Report order is by Date. Report is printed with Accounts having Zero Amounts and with Truncated Transaction Descriptions and in Detail Format

Date	Account ID	Reference	Trans Description	Debit Amt	Credit Amt
3/31/04	5530	Adjustments	Record Adjusting Journal Entries	600.00	
	1140		Record Adjusting Journal Entries		600.00
	5550		Record Adjusting Journal Entries	150.00	
	1251		Record Adjusting Journal Entries		150.00
	2400		Record Adjusting Journal Entries	200.00	
	4600		Record Adjusting Journal Entries		200.00
		Total		950.00	950.00

b.   General Ledger Trial Balance

```
                                              The Corner Dress Shop
                                          General Ledger Trial Balance
                                              As of Mar 31, 2004
Filter Criteria includes: Report order is by ID. Report is printed in Detail Format.
```

Account ID	Account Description	Debit Amt	Credit Amt
1110	Cash	26,587.35	
1115	Petty Cash	35.00	
1120	Accounts Receivable	15,000.00	
1130	Inventory	13,515.00	
1135	Inventory-Purchase Discounts		280.00
1140	Prepaid Rent	1,200.00	
1250	Delivery Truck	23,200.00	
1251	Accum. Dep-Delivery Truck		1,650.00
2110	Accounts Payable		39,100.00
2310	Federal Income Tax Payable		1,382.09
2320	State Income Tax Payable		577.08
2330	FICA- Soc. Sec. Payable		1,513.42
2335	FICA- Medicare Payable		353.94
2340	FUTA Payable		260.84
2350	SUTA Payable		1,565.04
2400	Unearned Rent		600.00
3110	Betty Loeb, Capital		9,103.10
3120	Betty Loeb, Withdrawals	100.00	
4110	Sales		69,200.00
4140	Sales Discounts	160.00	
4600	Rental Income		200.00
5050	Cost of Goods Sold	31,085.00	
5100	Delivery Expense	10.00	
5400	Salaries Expense	12,205.00	
5420	Payroll Tax Expense	1,617.16	
5500	Postage Expense	5.00	
5510	Cleaning Expense	306.00	
5530	Rent Expense	600.00	
5550	Depreciation Exp.-Truck	150.00	
5560	Miscellaneous Expense	10.00	
	Total:	125,785.51	125,785.51

c.   General Ledger Report

```
                                              The Corner Dress Shop
                                               General Ledger
                                     For the Period From Mar 1, 2004 to Mar 31, 2004
Filter Criteria includes: Report order is by ID. Report is printed with Truncated Transaction Descriptions and in Detail Format.
```

Account ID Account Description	Date	Reference	Jrnl	Trans Description	Debit Amt	Credit Amt	Balance
1110	3/1/04			Beginning Balance			2,502.90
Cash	3/1/04	7634	CRJ	Bing Company	2,200.00		
	3/10/04	110	CDJ	Rhonda's Cleaning Ser		300.00	
	3/12/04	111	CDJ	Morris Company		9,800.00	
	3/13/04	Cash	CRJ	Cash	7,000.00		
	3/15/04	112	CDJ	Internal Revenue Servi		2,936.40	
	3/15/04	Cash	CRJ	Cash	29,000.00		
	3/15/04	113	CDJ	Betty Loeb		100.00	
	3/15/04	114	CDJ	State of Massachusetts		756.00	
	3/17/04	5432	CRJ	Ronold Company	3,920.00		
	3/17/04	5447	CRJ	Ronold Company	7,000.00		
	3/23/04	115	CDJ	Jones Company		7,920.00	
	3/25/04	116	CDJ	Jones Company		1,000.00	
	3/28/04	5562	CRJ	Ronold Company	3,920.00		
	3/28/04	8127	CRJ	Bing Company	3,200.00		
	3/30/04	117	CDJ	Cash		31.00	
	3/31/04	118	PRJ	Mel Case		2,633.97	
	3/31/04	119	PRJ	Jane Holl		3,164.85	
	3/31/04	120	PRJ	Jackie Moore		3,513.33	
				Current Period Change	56,240.00	32,155.55	24,084.45
	3/31/04			Ending Balance			26,587.35
1115	3/1/04			Beginning Balance			35.00
Petty Cash	3/31/04			Ending Balance			35.00
1120	3/1/04			Beginning Balance			2,200.00
Accounts Receivable	3/1/04	7634	CRJ	Bing Company - Invoi		2,200.00	
	3/3/04	51	SJ	Ronold Company	7,000.00		

d.   Balance Sheet

```
                                          The Corner Dress Shop
                                             Balance Sheet
                                            March 31, 2004

                                               ASSETS

Current Assets
Cash                              $        26,587.35
Petty Cash                                     35.00
Accounts Receivable                        15,000.00
Inventory                                  13,515.00
Inventory-Purchase Discounts                 (280.00)
Prepaid Rent                                1,200.00

Total Current Assets                                      56,057.35

Property and Equipment
Delivery Truck                             23,200.00
Accum. Dep-Delivery Truck                  (1,650.00)

Total Property and Equipment                             21,550.00

Other Assets

Total Other Assets                                            0.00

Total Assets                      $                      77,607.35


                                       LIABILITIES AND CAPITAL

Current Liabilities
Accounts Payable                  $        39,100.00
Federal Income Tax Payable                  1,382.09
State Income Tax Payable                      577.08
FICA- Soc. Sec. Payable                     1,513.42
```

e. Income Statement

```
                                          The Corner Dress Shop
                                            Income Statement
                                 For the Three Months Ending March 31, 2004

                            Current Month                    Year to Date
Revenues
Sales                 $      69,200.00    99.94   $      69,200.00    99.94
Sales Discounts               (160.00)   (0.23)            (160.00)   (0.23)
Rental Income                  200.00     0.29              200.00     0.29

Total Revenues               69,240.00   100.00          69,240.00   100.00


Cost of Sales
Cost of Goods Sold           31,085.00    44.89          31,085.00    44.89

Total Cost of Sales          31,085.00    44.89          31,085.00    44.89

Gross Profit                 38,155.00    55.11          38,155.00    55.11

Expenses
Delivery Expense                 10.00     0.01               10.00     0.01
Salaries Expense             12,205.00    17.63          12,205.00    17.63
Payroll Tax Expense           1,617.16     2.34           1,617.16     2.34
Postage Expense                   5.00     0.01                5.00     0.01
Cleaning Expense                306.00     0.44              306.00     0.44
Rent Expense                    600.00     0.87              600.00     0.87
Depreciation Exp.-Truck         150.00     0.22              150.00     0.22
Miscellaneous Expense            10.00     0.01               10.00     0.01

Total Expenses               14,903.16    21.52          14,903.16    21.52

Net Income            $      23,251.84    33.58   $      23,251.84    33.58
```

f. Inventory Valuation Report

The Corner Dress Shop							
Inventory Valuation Report							
As of Mar 31, 2004							
Filter Criteria includes: 1) Stock/Assembly. Report order is by ID. Report is printed with Truncated Long Descriptions.							

Item ID Item Class	Item Description	Stocking U/M	Cost Method	Qty on Hand	Item Value	Avg Cost	% of Inv Value
1000 Stock item	Dress, Style 1000	Each	Average	160.00	4,450.00	27.81	32.93
2000 Stock item	Dress, Style 2000	Each	Average	167.00	5,310.00	31.80	39.29
3000 Stock item	Dress, Style 3000	Each	Average	12.00	420.00	35.00	3.11
4000 Stock item	Dress, Style 4000	Each	Average	8.00	320.00	40.00	2.37
5000 Stock item	Dress, Style 5000	Each	Average	27.00	1,215.00	45.00	8.99
6000 Stock item	Dress, Style 6000	Each	Average	36.00	1,800.00	50.00	13.32
					13,515.00		100.00

10. Compare the Inventory Valuation Report with the one created at the start of this practice set. Note that the first two items, the ones whose cost price changed when we last purchased them, have neither the original prices of $25.00 and $30.00 nor the new prices of $28.00 and $32.00 respectively. Peachtree has created a weighted-average for these items.

Advance Dates

11. In order to close the accounting period we must now advance the period.

♦ Using your mouse, click on **System** from the **Tasks** menu. Select **Change Accounting Period**.

♦ Using the list at left, select 04- Apr 1, 2004 to Apr 30, 2004 and click on "Ok"

♦ You will be asked whether you wish to print reports before continuing. Since we have already printed our reports, we can answer "No".

♦ Note that the status bar at the bottom of the screen now reflects that you are in period 4. You would be ready to start recording the April transactions.

12. You should back up your work after each chapter following instructions in Chapter 1.

13. Click on File and select Exit to end the current work session

CHAPTER 8

Working With A Perpetual Inventory System - The Paint Place Mini Practice Set

Before starting on this assignment, read and complete Chapters 1 through 6.

Perpetual Inventory Overview

One of the most powerful features of a computerized accounting system is its ability to maintain perpetual inventory records easily and accurately. In the prior Peachtree Workshops this feature was demonstrated as you recorded purchases and sales of inventory. Peachtree Complete Accounting 2005 has the ability to maintain perpetual inventory records through its Inventory module. Peachtree Complete Accounting 2005 can use FIFO, LIFO or the weighted-average method as its inventory cost flow assumption. While a default assumption can be set, one can be designated for each inventory item individually.

In this Computer Workshop you will be working with the data files for a company called The Paint Place. The Paint Place uses the Sales/Invoicing, Receipts, Purchases, Payments and Inventory modules of Peachtree Complete Accounting 2005 to maintain its accounting and perpetual inventory records. The Paint Place extends terms of 2/10, n/30 to all of its credit customers. The inventory items currently stocked by The Paint Place appear below:

Inventory List

The Paint Place
Inventory Synopsis 3/1/04

No.	Description	Unit	Sell	Quantity	Cost	Value	Margin (%)
1	Latex Flat	Gallon	16.95	642	7.47	4,795.74	55.93
2	Latex Semi-gloss	Gallon	16.95	1,066	7.47	7,963.02	55.93
3	Latex High-gloss	Gallon	16.95	600	7.47	4,482.00	55.93
4	Oil High-gloss	Gallon	17.95	801	8.97	7,184.97	50.03
5	Oil Semi-gloss	Gallon	17.95	502	8.97	4,502.94	50.03
						28,928.67	

Open the Company Data Files

1. Double click on the Peachtree Complete Accounting 2005 icon on your desktop to open the software program.

2. Open the existing company file for **The Paint Place**.

   You should back up your work before starting each chapter following instructions in Chapter 1.

Add Your Name to the company Name

3. Click on the **Maintain** menu option. Then select **Company Information**. The program will respond by bringing up a dialogue box allowing the user to edit/add information about the company. In the **Company Name** entry field at the end of **The Paint Place**, add a dash and your name "**-Student Name**" to the end of the company name. Click the OK button.

4. Peachtree Complete Accounting 2005 allows the user to quickly and easily add new inventory items to the Inventory module. This is accomplished by selecting **Inventory Items** from the **Maintain** menu. From this window, we can also obtain and edit information about items currently in our inventory. To illustrate how easily inventory items can be added, let's add a new product to the **The Paint Place** inventory module.

♦ Select **Inventory Items** from the **Maintain** menu.

♦ In the **Item ID** field, type "006"and hit TAB.

♦ In the **Description** field, type in "Oil Flat" and hit TAB.

♦ We are now in a field where we can change the type of inventory item this is. Since this will be a regular stocked item, we can accept the default of Stock Item by hitting TAB twice.

♦ We are now in a field where we can enter a longer description of this item that will appear on sales and/or purchase invoices when we select it. Since we do not have a longer description, we can TAB until we reach the **Price Level 1** field.

♦ We will sell this item normally for $16.95 so enter this amount.

♦ Peachtree has the capability of storing multiple prices for an item. This feature can be activated by clicking on the arrow to the right of the **Price Level 1** field. Go ahead and click on this arrow. A table is presented which allows us to enter up to 10 different selling prices. Different customers can be given different price levels in this manner. Since we will have only one price, we can **Cancel** the Multiple Price Level box.

♦ TAB until you reach **Cost Method**. Here is where we can select the cost assumption to use with this item. We will select "Average". Note that we could select FIFO or LIFO at this point.

♦ Item Type and Location are information fields that we will not use at this time

♦ TAB to Stocking U/M (Unit/Measure) field. The paint is sold in 1 gallon cans, type in "Gallon" in this field. Hit TAB to move to the next field.

♦ Peachtree has used default information to select the GL accounts needed for an inventory transaction. Unless there is some need to change these, we will accept the defaults. In fact, we will accept Peachtree's default information on the rest of the accounts in this field. We will also not use the **Custom Fields** or **History** tabs in this window. Your screen should look like this:

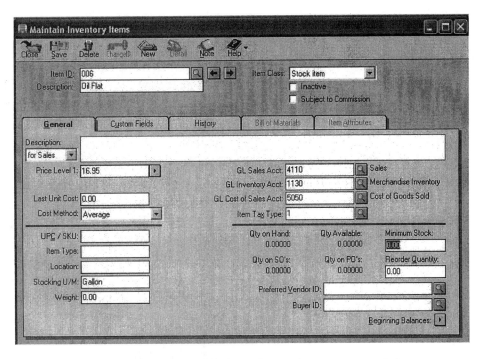

♦ Clicking on **Save** will place this item in our inventory module.

♦ We can view and edit information about items in our inventory from this window as well. We can use the magnifying glass next to the **Item ID** field to select any item from our inventory by double clicking on it. Once it is in the Maintain Inventory Items box, we can click on and change information as needed.

Record Transactions

5. Using the procedures learned in Chapter 6, record the following transactions using the appropriate General (G), Sales/Invoicing (S), Receipts(R), Purchases/Receive Inventory (PU), and Payments (PA) windows. Accept defaults for any fields for which you are not given information. Remember to use the Plain Invoice format for sales invoices and to insert the invoice number during the printing process for all print activities:

2004

Mar. 1 Sold 5 gallons of Oil High-gloss (Item #4) at $17.95 per gallon to Elaine Anderson on account, invoice no. 5469, $89.75, terms 2/10, n/30. [S]

3 Received invoice no. 6892 from Wholesale Paints in the amount of $1,504 for the purchase of 200 gallons of Latex High-gloss (Item #3) at $7.52 per gallon, (don't forget to change the **Unit Price**), terms 2/10, n/30. [PU]

3 Received invoice no. CC675 from the Painter's Supply in the amount of $906 for the purchase of 100 gallons of Oil High-gloss (Item #4) at 9.06 per gallon (don't forget to change the **Unit Price**), terms 2/10, n/30. [PU]

4 Sold 5 gallons of Oil High-gloss paint (Item #4) at $17.95 per gallon to Jake Kerns on account, invoice no. 5470, $89.75, terms 2/10, n/30. [S]

6 Received check no. 8723 from Wes Young in the amount of $3,225.13 in payment of invoice no. 5468 ($3,290.95), dated February 28, less 2 percent discount ($65.82).

Receipt No. 101. [R]

7   Issued check no. 2345 to Vantage Tints in the amount of $1,082.84 in payment of invoice no. 5658 ($1,116.33), dated February 28, less 3 percent discount ($33.49). [PA]

14   Sold 10 gallons of Latex Semi-gloss (Item #2) at $16.95 per gallon to Elaine Anderson on account, $169.50, invoice no. 5471, terms 2/10, n/30. [S]

17   Received invoice no. 6943 from Wholesale Paints in the amount of $1,134 for the purchase of 150 gallons of Latex Semi-gloss (Item #2) at 7.56 per gallon (don't forget to change the **Unit Price**), terms 2/10, n/30. [PU]

19   Received invoice no. CC691 from Painter's Supply in the amount of $1,618.75 for the purchase of 175 gallons of Oil Semi-gloss (Item #5) at 9.25 per gallon (don't forget to change the **Unit Price**), terms 2/10, n/30. [PU]

21   Sold 10 gallons of Latex Semi-gloss (Item #2) at $16.95 per gallon to Jake Kerns on account, $169.50, invoice no. 5472, terms 2/10, n/30. [S]

24   Sold 25 gallons of Oil Semi-gloss paint (Item #5) at $17.95 per gallon to Elaine Anderson on account, $448.75, invoice no. 5473, terms 2/10, n/30. [S]

25   Received invoice no. CC787 from Painter's Supply in the amount of $465 for the purchase of 50 gallons of Oil Semi-gloss (Item #5) at 9.30 per gallon (don't forget to change the **Unit Price**), terms 2/10, n/30. [PU]

31   Sold 25 gallons of Oil Semi-gloss (Item #5) at $17.95 per gallon to Jake Kerns on account, $448.75, invoice no. 5474, terms 2/10, n/30. [S]

How to Display an Inventory Activity Detail Report

6. You may wish to see how active the items in your inventory have been. Peachtree has a Unit Activity Report that will summarize the units bought for any selected period. Select **Inventory** from the **Reports** menu. Select **Inventory Unit Activity Report**. Accept all defaults. Your screen will look like this:

The Paint Place-Student Name
Inventory Unit Activity Report
For the Period From Mar 1, 2004 to Mar 31, 2004
Filter Criteria includes: 1) Stock/Assembly. Report order is by ID. Report is printed with Truncated Long Descriptions.

Item ID Item Description Item Class	Beg Qty	Units Sold	Units Purc	Adjust Qty	Assembly Qty	Qty on Hand
001 Latex Flat Stock item	642.00					642.00
002 Latex Semi-Gloss Stock item	1066.00	20.00	150.00			1196.00
003 Latex High-Gloss Stock item	600.00		200.00			800.00
004 Oil High-Gloss Stock item	801.00	10.00	100.00			891.00
005 Oil Semi-Gloss Stock item	502.00	50.00	225.00			677.00
006 Oil Flat Stock item						
		80.00	675.00			

7. An important inventory report is the Inventory Valuation Report. From the same report screen, select Inventory Valuation report and accept all defaults. Your screen will look like this:

The Paint Place-Student Name
Inventory Valuation Report
As of Mar 31, 2004
Filter Criteria includes: 1) Stock/Assembly. Report order is by ID. Report is printed with Truncated Long Descriptions.

Item ID Item Class	Item Description	Stocking U/M	Cost Method	Qty on Hand	Item Value	Avg Cost	% of Inv Value
001 Stock item	Latex Flat	Gallon	Average	642.00	4,795.74	7.47	14.16
002 Stock item	Latex Semi-Gloss	Gallon	Average	1196.00	8,947.51	7.48	26.42
003 Stock item	Latex High-Gloss	Gallon	Average	800.00	5,986.00	7.48	17.68
004 Stock item	Oil High-Gloss	Gallon	Average	891.00	8,001.22	8.98	23.63
005 Stock item	Oil Semi-Gloss	Gallon	Average	677.00	6,134.11	9.06	18.11
006 Stock item	Oil Flat	Gallon	Average				
					33,864.58		100.00

8. As you can see from the report menu, there are numerous other reports Peachtree can utilize. These are outside the scope of this book.

9. Print the following reports accepting all defaults:

   a. General Ledger Trial Balance

Filter Criteria includes: Report order is by ID. Report is printed in Detail Format.

Account ID	Account Description	Debit Amt	Credit Amt
1110	Cash	26,015.23	
1120	Accounts Receivable	6,385.00	
1130	Merchandise Inventory	33,018.01	
1140	Prepaid Rent	2,200.00	
1150	Store Supplies	1,622.30	
1250	Office Equipment	12,800.00	
1251	Accum. Dep-Office Equipment		1,469.44
1350	Store Equipment	13,500.00	
1351	Accum. Dep- Store Equipment		1,916.67
2110	Accounts Payable		8,653.54
3110	Mike Poole, Capital		37,728.86
3130	Retained Earnings		41,822.74
4110	Sales		4,706.95
4140	Sales Discounts	65.82	
5050	Cost of Goods Sold	691.84	
	Total:	96,298.20	96,298.20

b. Aged Receivables

Filter Criteria includes: Report order is by ID. Report is printed in Detail Format.

Customer ID / Customer / Contact / Telephone 1	Invoice/CM #	0-30	31-60	61-90	Over 90 days	Amount Due
001	5441	2,293.05				2,293.05
Elaine Anderson	5469	89.75				89.75
	5471	169.50				169.50
	5473	448.75				448.75
001		3,001.05				3,001.05
Elaine Anderson						
002	5461	2,675.95				2,675.95
Jake Kerns	5470	89.75				89.75
	5472	169.50				169.50
	5474	448.75				448.75
002		3,383.95				3,383.95
Jake Kerns						
Report Total		6,385.00				6,385.00

c. Aged Payables

Filter Criteria includes: Report order is by ID. Report is printed in Detail Format.

Vendor ID Vendor Contact Telephone 1	Invoice/CM #	0 - 30	31 - 60	61 - 90	Over 90 days	Amount Due
001	4356	975.34				975.34
Painter's Supply	CC675	906.00				906.00
	CC691	1,618.75				1,618.75
	CC787	465.00				465.00
001 Painter's Supply		3,965.09				3,965.09
003	56780	2,050.45				2,050.45
Wholesale Paints	6892	1,504.00				1,504.00
	6943	1,134.00				1,134.00
003 Wholesale Paints		4,688.45				4,688.45
Report Total		8,653.54				8,653.54

d. Income Statement

	Current Month		Year to Date	
Revenues				
Sales	$ 1,416.00	104.87	$ 4,706.95	101.42
Sales Returns & Allowances	0.00	0.00	0.00	0.00
Sales Discounts	(65.82)	(4.87)	(65.82)	(1.42)
Total Revenues	1,350.18	100.00	4,641.13	100.00
Cost of Sales				
Cost of Goods Sold	691.84	51.24	691.84	14.91
Total Cost of Sales	691.84	51.24	691.84	14.91
Gross Profit	658.34	48.76	3,949.29	85.09
Expenses				
Delivery Expense	0.00	0.00	0.00	0.00
Advertising Expense	0.00	0.00	0.00	0.00
Utilities Expense	0.00	0.00	0.00	0.00
Store Supplies Expense	0.00	0.00	0.00	0.00
Rent Expense	0.00	0.00	0.00	0.00
Deprec Exp.: Office Equipment	0.00	0.00	0.00	0.00
Deprec Exp.: Store Equipment	0.00	0.00	0.00	0.00
Miscellaneous Expense	0.00	0.00	0.00	0.00
Total Expenses	0.00	0.00	0.00	0.00
Net Income	$ 658.34	48.76	$ 3,949.29	85.09

e. Balance Sheet

```
                                          The Paint Place-Student Name
                                                Balance Sheet
                                               March 31, 2004
                                                    ASSETS

Current Assets
Cash                              $        26,015.23
Accounts Receivable                         6,385.00
Merchandise Inventory                      33,018.01
Prepaid Rent                                2,200.00
Store Supplies                              1,622.30

Total Current Assets                                         69,240.54

Property and Equipment
Office Equipment                           12,800.00
Accum. Dep-Office Equipment                (1,469.44)
Store Equipment                            13,500.00
Accum. Dep- Store Equipment                (1,916.67)

Total Property and Equipment                                22,913.89

Other Assets

Total Other Assets                                               0.00

Total Assets                      $                         92,154.43


                                          LIABILITIES AND CAPITAL

Current Liabilities
Accounts Payable                  $         8,653.54
```

10. You should back up your work after each chapter following instructions in Chapter 1.

Exit from the Program

11. Click on the File menu; then click on Exit to end the current work session and return to your Windows desktop.

CHAPTER 9

Financial Analysis with Peachtree

Before starting on this assignment, read and complete Chapter 1

Computers and accounting programs like Peachtree Complete Accounting 2005 have revolutionized the generation of accounting reports for managers. Before their widespread introduction into the business world, many businesses were forced to painstakingly create their reports by hand. Today, most reports are as simple as a few mouse clicks. Peachtree contains over 100 reports in standard format. In addition, you can create custom reports for any data which is kept by Peachtree. The power of this reporting system allows the user to analyze the financial postion of the company quickly and easily.

In this chapter, you are not completing a specific workshop but rather are invited to open a company and explore the various reports that Peachtree can generate for this company. As each report area is discussed, please feel free to look at the reports available for the sample company within the area.

Open the Company Data Files

1. Double click on the Peachtree Complete Accounting 2005 icon on your desktop.

2. Open the existing company file for **Bellwether Garden Supply**.

   You should back up your work before starting each chapter following instructions in Chapter 1.

Add Your Name to the company Name

3. Click on the **Maintain** menu option. Then select **Company Information**. The program will respond by bringing up a dialogue box allowing the user to edit/add information about the company. In the **Company Name** entry field at the end of open **Bellwether Garden Supply**, add a dash and your name "**-Student Name**" or initials to the end of the company name. Click on the OK button to return to the Menu Window.

The Reports Menu

4. Peachtree has many existing reports plus the ability to create virtually any report needed. The **R**eports pull down menu contains 14 separate items:

```
┌─────────────────────────────┐
│   Accounts Receivable...    │
│   Accounts Payable...       │
│   Payroll...                │
├─────────────────────────────┤
│   General Ledger...         │
│   Financial Statements...   │
├─────────────────────────────┤
│   Inventory...              │
│   Jobs...                   │
│   Account Reconciliation... │
├─────────────────────────────┤
│   Time/Expense...           │
│   Company...                │
│   Mail Merge...             │
├─────────────────────────────┤
│   Report Groups...          │
│   Report Styles...          │
│   My Business...            │
│   Daily Register...         │
└─────────────────────────────┘
```

Each of the first nine **Reports** menu areas allows us to select, customize and print both reports and forms associated with each listed function. As an example, the Accounts Payable area allows not only those reports associated with Accounts Payable such as Aged Payables, but it will also allow us to print checks, 1099's, purchase orders and other activities. Let's look at some of the areas that should be familiar to you.

Accounts Receivable Reports

5. The Accounts Receivable option provides access to the various reports that one would associate with Sales. They provide us with information about our customers, our prospective customers, the invoices we generated, the moneys owed to us by our customers, cash receipts and reports detailing how Peachtree processed transactions related to our Sales. In addition to the 19 standard reports, there are also 8 folders of forms or other printed documents available within the Accounts Receivable reports function. Any of these items not already explored in other chapters of the book can be and should be explored now. Some reports may not contain any data while others are not appropriate for this particular business.

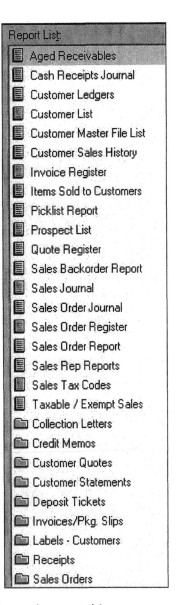

Report List:
- Aged Receivables
- Cash Receipts Journal
- Customer Ledgers
- Customer List
- Customer Master File List
- Customer Sales History
- Invoice Register
- Items Sold to Customers
- Picklist Report
- Prospect List
- Quote Register
- Sales Backorder Report
- Sales Journal
- Sales Order Journal
- Sales Order Register
- Sales Order Report
- Sales Rep Reports
- Sales Tax Codes
- Taxable / Exempt Sales
- Collection Letters
- Credit Memos
- Customer Quotes
- Customer Statements
- Deposit Tickets
- Invoices/Pkg. Slips
- Labels - Customers
- Receipts
- Sales Orders

Accounts Payable Reports

6. The Accounts Payable option provides access to various reports that are associate with the purchase of goods or services. They provide us with information about our vendor, the invoices we receive, the moneys owed by us to our vendors, cash payments and reports detailing how Peachtree processed transactions related to purchase of goods and services within both the General and Subsidiary Ledgers. In addition to the 12 reports, there are also 4 folders of forms or other printed documents available within the Accounts Payable reports function. Any of these items not already explored in other chapters of the book can be and should be explored by the student now. Some reports may not contain any data while others are not appropriate for this particular business.

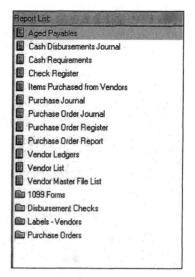

Payroll Reports

7. This area provides access to various reports that are associated with Payroll. The provide us with information about our employees and their earnings, the paychecks we generate, payroll taxes and reports detailing how Peachtree has processed transactions related to Payroll within the General Ledger. In addition to the 10 reports, there are also 6 folders of forms or other printed documents available within the Payroll reports function. Any of these items not already explored in other chapters of the book can be and should be explored by the student now. Some reports may not contain any data while others are not appropriate for this particular business.

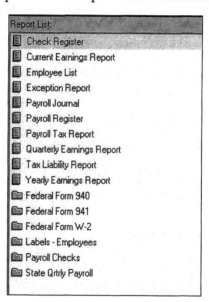

General Ledger Reports

8. This area provides access to the various reports that are associated with the General Ledger. They provide us with information about our Chart of Accounts, the balances in our accounts, the activity in each Ledger account and reports detailing how Peachtree processed transactions as they were posted to the General Ledger. There are no folders with forms or other reports available in this area. The General Ledger reports are important audit tools as they can furnish us with all the debits and credits for any account in our General Ledger. That makes finding errors quick and easy.

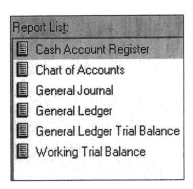

Financial Statement Reports

9. This area provides access to the various reports that are associated with the Financial Statements. They provided us with information about our Assets, Liabilities, Owner's Equity, Expenses, Revenues, Budgets and provide comparisons for various items within the General Ledger. There are no folders with forms or other documents available in this area. Many of these statements are set up to provide us with comparisons from year to year, actual to budget and other important comparisons used in financial analysis. In addition, the income statements are shown with vertical analysis percents already calculated. Be sure to look at the cash flow report to see how quickly and easily Peachtree can generate this difficult to create report.

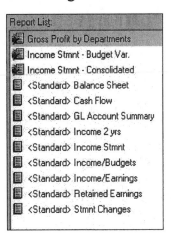

10. Other Reports areas are:

   ♦ **Inventory** - Provides numerous reports to assist in managing merchandise inventory.

   ♦ **Job Reports** - Provides reports associated with specific jobs and the costs to perform those jobs. Useful in situations which call for job costing.

   ♦ **Account Reconciliation** - Provides reports associated with the reconciliation of our cash account. Also allows printouts of Deposits, Outstanding Checks, Deposits in Transit and other uncleared items.

   ♦ **Time/Expense Reports** - detail time and expense transactions (tickets) used in the Time & Billing areas of Peachtree Accounting.

   ♦ **Report Groups** - Allows the user to set up a variety of reports from any of the major categories into one report group name for batch printing rather than selecting the reports one by one and printing them.

♦ **Company Reports** - Company reports detail audit trail information as data is entered, changed or deleted in your Peachtree Accounting company.

♦ **Reports Groups** - The Report Groups window displays the report groups that you have created. It allows you to group reports, financial statements, and views together so that you can print them in a batch. Report groups are helpful when you need to print the same grouping of reports every time.

As always, these features should be explored as you find time and the need so as to become familiar with their location and use.

CHAPTER 10

Notes Receivable and Notes Payable

Before starting on this assignment, read and complete Chapters 1 & 2

Peachtree Accounting does not have a specific provision for the recording of promissory notes from either the buyer's or the seller's prospective. Essentially what we must do is force Peachtree to accomplish these tasks for us. Generally speaking, Promissory Note entries that do not involve Accounts Receivable or Accounts Payable, such as cash loans, can be entered through the General Journal Entry window. However, entries that do involve these accounts must be entered through a window that will also perform a posting to the appropriate Subsidiary Ledger such as the Payments window or Receipts window. Using these entry windows allows us to maintain the balance between the Subsidiary Ledgers and their controlling accounts in the General Ledger, something that would not occur if we were to use a General Journal entry.

Peachtree will not automatically calculate interest and you will still be required to calculate interest manually.

Open the Company Data Files

1. Double click on the Peachtree Complete Accounting 2005 icon on your desktop.

2. Open the existing company data file for **Lundquist Custom Woodworking**.

   You should back up your work before starting each chapter following instructions in Chapter 1.

Add Your Name to the Company Name

3. Click on the **Maintain** menu option. Then select **Company Information**. The program will respond by bringing up a dialogue box allowing the user to edit/add information about the company. In the **Company Name** entry field at the end of **Lundquist Custom Woodworking**, add a dash and your name **"-Student Name"** to the end of the company name. Click on the OK button to return to the Menu Window.

Recording Notes Receivable

4. A common reason for issuing a promissory note is to use the note to extend the amount of time for settlement of an account receivable. To illustrate how easily notes can be added, let's add a new Note Receivable to **Lundquist Custom Woodworking**.

5. What we must do is move the amount owed to us from one asset account (Accounts Receivable) to another asset account (Notes Receivable). While we could accomplish this in Peachtree quickly and easily with a General Journal entry, the balance owed to us would continue to show in the Subsidiary Accounts Receivable Ledger. Instead of using the General Journal entry window, we will use the Receipts window, changing the debit to Cash into a debit to Notes Receivable. Let us assume that Betty's

Boutique, a customer of **Lundquist Custom Woodworking**, wishes to settle her accounts receivable by issuing a 12% 60-day note.

♦ Select **Receipts** from the **Tasks** menu.

♦ Remove the entry in the **Deposit ticket ID** field and enter "081504".

♦ Using the Lookup feature, select Betty's Boutique in the **Customer ID** field.

♦ In the **Reference** field, type "12%, 60 Day".

♦ In the **Receipt Number** field, type "101".

♦ In the **Date** field enter or select "8/15/04" as the date and press TAB.

♦ Using the mouse and the Lookup feature, select account 1130 Notes Receivable in the field marked **Cash Account**. This will force the debit to account 1130 instead of the cash account, 1110.

♦ Click on the **Apply to Invoices** tab.

♦ In the **Pay** column, select the $4,000 invoice by clicking in the box.

♦ Your screen should look like this:

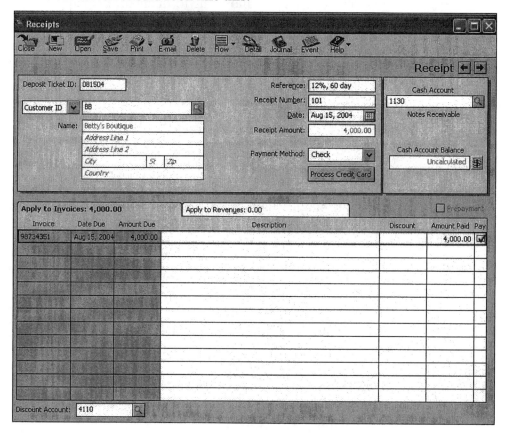

♦ Click on **Save** to complete the transaction.

♦ To view the impact of your transaction on the Subsidiary Accounts Receivable Ledger, you may look at an Aged Receivables report from the Accounts Receivable Report menu. You will note the invoice is no longer listed on this report. To view the impact on the General Ledger, you can look at the Cash Receipts Journal found in the same menu.

These reports can be viewed on your screen or printed for later examination.

> *Important Warning:* **By changing the Cash account to 1130, you will cause Peachtree to use this account number again in the next transaction entered through the Receipts window. Be sure to change the Cash account back to 1110 the next time this window is used.**

Recording Notes Payable

6. When one business records a promissory note as a notes receivable, another business will be recording the same note as a notes payable. This company, known as the maker of the note, is extending the time it has for payment of debt. What we are essentially doing is moving the amount we owe from one liability account (Accounts Payable) to another liability account (Notes Payable). Again we could accomplish this with a General Journal entry but we are faced with the problem of having the Subsidiary Ledger out of balance with the General Ledger. To prevent this, we will use the Payments window, changing the credit to Cash into a credit to Notes Payable.

7. To illustrate this, let us assume that we wish to extend the time for payment of our invoice to Elmer Lumber Supply. **Lundquist Custom Woodworking** will settle its accounts payable by issuing a 12% 60-day note.

   ♦ Select **Payments** from the **Tasks** menu.

   ♦ Using the Lookup feature, select Elmer Lumber Supply in the **Vendor ID** field.

   ♦ In the **Check Number** field, type "NP01" and TAB to the **Date** field.

   ♦ Enter or select 8/18/04 as the date and press TAB.

   ♦ In the **Memo** field, enter "12% 60 Day".

   ♦ Using the mouse and the Lookup feature, select account 2130 Notes Payable in the field marked **Cash Account**. This will force the credit to account 2130 instead of account 1110.

   ♦ Click on the **Apply to Invoices** tab.

   ♦ In the **Pay** column, select the $800 invoice by clicking in the box.

   ♦ Your screen should look like this:

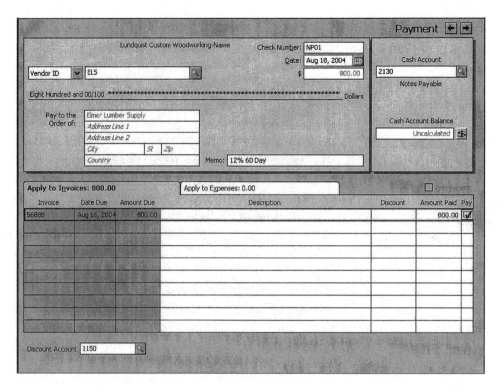

- ◆ Click on **Save** to complete the transaction.

- ◆ To view the impact of your transaction on the Subsidiary Accounts Payable Ledger, you may look at an Aged Payables report from the Accounts Payable Report menu. You will note the invoice is no longer listed on this report. To view the impact on the General Ledger, you can look at the Cash Disbursements Journal found in the same menu. These reports can be viewed on your screen or printed for later examination.

> *Important Warning:* **By changing the Cash account to 2130, you will cause Peachtree to use this account number again in the next transaction entered through the Payments window. Be sure to change the Cash account back to 1110 the next time this window is used.**

Recording Cash Receipt of a Note Receivable

8. Once recorded, the promissory note no longer has an impact on our subsidiary ledgers. We could, therefore, record the payment of the note in our General Journal; however, cash receipts collected for our Notes Receivables are best entered through the Receipts window and cash payments paid on our Notes Payables are best made through the Payments window. Peachtree will not calculate the interest for us. We accomplish this in precisely the same manner as we would in a manual accounting system by using the formula: $I = P \times R \times T$

9. To illustrate the receipt of cash for an existing Note Receivable, let us assume that payment has been received for an existing Note Receivable with a principle value in the amount of $5,000.00. **Lundquist Custom Woodworking** accepted a 12% 30-day note on 21 July 2004. It is now 20 August 2004, 30 days later and payment in full has been received. Interest earned would be $I = \$5,000.00 \times 12\% \times 30/360 = \$50.00$.

- ◆ Select **Receipts** from the **Tasks** menu.

- ◆ Since the cash received must be deposited, for the **Deposit Ticket ID field** and enter "082004". Press TAB.

- ◆ Since this payment is not a payment on an Accounts Receivable, we cannot use the **Customer ID** field. We will use instead, the **Name** field to record the name of the party who is paying the Note. Enter "Erin's Designs" in the Name field. Hit TAB.

- ◆ In the **Reference** field, enter "1501", the number of the check Erin has sent us, and TAB to Receipt Number.

- ◆ In the **Receipt Number** field, type "102".

- ◆ Enter or select "8/20/04" as the date and press TAB.

- ◆ Accept the default of "Check" in the **Payment Method** field. Press TAB.

- ◆ In the **Cash Account** field, make sure it contains 1110, our cash account. (It may still be set to 1130 Notes Receivable from our prior transaction.)

- ◆ Click in the **Description** column of the first row and type "Payment for note receivable". TAB to the GL column.

- ◆ Using the Lookup feature, select account 1130 Notes Receivable since we are applying this cash receipt in part to the Notes Receivable account. TAB to the **Amount** column.

- ◆ Enter "5000" into the **Amount** column which was the original amount of the note. TAB to the **Description** column in the next row.

- ◆ Type "Interest revenue" in the **Description** column and TAB to the GL column.

- ◆ Using the Lookup feature, select account 4200 Interest Revenue and TAB to the **Amount** column.

- ◆ Enter "50" in the Amount column. This was the amount we calculated using the interest formula.

- ◆ Your screen should look like this:

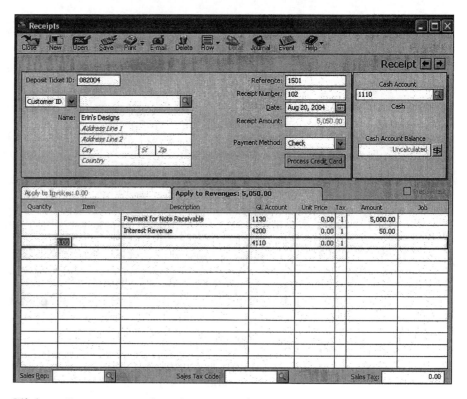

♦ Click on **Save** to complete the transaction.

Recording Cash Payment for a Note Payable

10. To illustrate the payment of cash for an existing Note Payable, let us assume that payment is being made for an existing Note Payable with a principle value in the amount of $3,000.00. We need to pay the liability and the interest expense that has accumulated since the note was issued. **Lundquist Custom Woodworking** issued a 12% 60-day note on 26 June 2004. It is now 25 August 2004, 60 days later and payment in full is being made. Interest expense would be I = $3,000.00 x 12% x 60/360 = $60.00.

♦ Select **Payments** from the **Tasks** menu.

♦ Since this payment is not a payment on an Accounts Payable, we cannot use the **Vendor ID** field. We will use instead, the **Pay to the Order of** field to record the name of the party who is being paid. Enter "Bank of Salinas" in the Pay to the order of field. Hit TAB until you reach the **Date** field.

♦ Enter or select "8/25/04" as the date and press TAB until you reach the **Cash Account** field.

♦ In the **Cash Account** field, make sure it contains 1110, our cash account. (It may still be set to 2130 Notes Payable from our prior transaction.)

♦ Click in the **Description** column of the first row and type "Payment of note payable". TAB to the GL column.

♦ Using the Lookup feature, select account 2130 Notes Payable since we are applying this cash payment in part to the Notes Payable account. TAB to the **Amount** column.

♦ Enter "3000" into the **Amount** column which was the original amount of the note. TAB to the **Description** column in the next row.

- ♦ Type "Interest expense" in the **Description** column and TAB to the GL column.

- ♦ Using the Lookup feature, select account 5200 Interest Expense and TAB to the **Amount** column.

- ♦ Enter "60" in the Amount column. This was the amount we calculated using the interest formula.

- ♦ Your screen should look like this:

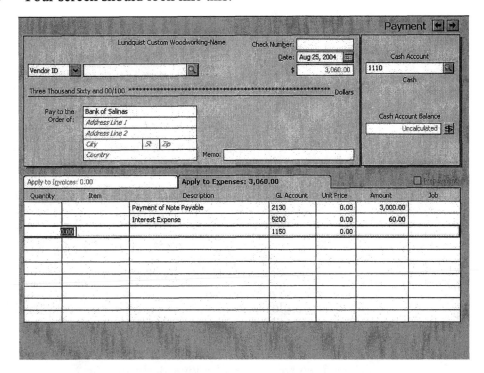

- ♦ After verifying that the check is correct, click on the Print icon to print this check. You will be presented with a Print Forms: Disbursement Checks selection box. Use the default form "MultiP APChks 1 Stub". Enter "103" as the check number and select Print. You should end up with a check made out to Bank of Salinas in the amount of $3,060.00. A blank Payment window is displayed, ready for additional Payments transactions to be recorded. Close the Payments dialog box.

11. There are many other situations that could involve Notes Payables or Notes Receivable. In every case, we would manipulate the Receipts and Payments windows of Peachtree to accommodate our needs.

12. You may examine Cash Receipts Journal and the Cash Payments Journal to view the impact of these transactions.

Lundquist Custom Woodworking-Name
Cash Receipts Journal
For the Period From Aug 1, 2004 to Aug 31, 2004

Filter Criteria includes: Report order is by Check Date. Report is printed in Detail Format.

Date	Account ID	Transaction Ref	Line Description	Debit Amnt	Credit Amnt
8/15/04	1120	12% 60 Day	Invoice: 98734351		4,000.00
	1130		Betty's Boutique	4,000.00	
8/20/04	1130	1501	Payment for Note Receivable		5,000.00
	4200		Interest Revenue		50.00
	1110		Erin's Designs	5,050.00	
				9,050.00	9,050.00

Lundquist Custom Woodworking-Name
Cash Disbursements Journal
For the Period From Aug 1, 2004 to Aug 31, 2004

Filter Criteria includes: Report order is by Date. Report is printed in Detail Format.

Date	Check #	Account ID	Line Description	Debit Amount	Credit Amount
8/18/04	NP01	2110	Invoice: 5688B	800.00	
		2130	Elmer Lumber Supply		800.00
8/25/04	103	2130	Payment of Note Payable	3,000.00	
		5200	Interest Expense	60.00	
		1110	Bank of Salinas		3,060.00
	Total			3,860.00	3,860.00

13. You should back up your work after each chapter following instructions in Chapter 1.

14. Click on the File menu; then click on Exit to end the current work session and return to your Windows desktop.

PART A
An Introduction to Computers and Peachtree

Accounting procedures are essentially the same whether they are performed manually or on a computer. The following is a list of the account cycle steps in a manual accounting system as compared to the steps in a computerized accounting system.

STEPS OF THE ACCOUNTING CYCLE

Manual Accounting System	Computerized Accounting System
1. Business transactions occur and generate source documents.	1. Business transactions occur and generate source documents.
2. Analyze and record business transactions in a manual journal.	2. Analyze and enter business transactions in a computerized journal.
3. Post or transfer information from journal to ledger.	3. Computer automatically posts information from journal to ledger.
4. Prepare a trial balance.	4. Trial balance is prepared automatically.
5. Prepare a worksheet.	5. Enter necessary adjustments directly.
6. Prepare financial statements.	6. Financial statements are prepared automatically.
7. Journalize and post adjusting entries.	7. Completed prior to preparation of financial statements.
8. Journalize and post closing entries.	8. Closing procedures are completed automatically.
9. Prepare a post-closing trial balance.	9. Trial balance is automatically prepared as needed.

The accounting cycle comparison shows that the accountant's task of initially analyzing business transactions in terms of debits and credits (both routine business transactions and adjusting entries) is required in both manual and computerized accounting systems. However, in a computerized accounting system, the "drudge" work of posting transactions, creating and completing worksheets and financial statements, and performing the closing procedures is all handled automatically by the computerized accounting system.

In addition, computerized accounting systems can perform accounting procedures at greater speeds and with greater accuracy than can be achieved in a manual accounting system. It is important to recognize, however, that the computer is only a tool that can accept and process information supplied by the accountant. Each business transaction and adjusting entry must first be analyzed and recorded in a computerized journal correctly; otherwise, the financial statements generated by the computerized accounting system will contain errors and will not be useful to the business.

COMPUTER SYSTEM

A computer system consists of several electronic components that together have the ability to accept user-supplied data; input, store, and execute programmed instructions; and output results according to use specifications. The physical computer and its related devices are the hardware, while the stored program that supplies the instructions is called the software.

COMPUTER SOFTWARE

The computer can do nothing without a computer program. Computer programs control the input, processing, storage, and output operations of a computer. Computer programmers write the instructions that tell the computer to execute certain procedures and process data. There are two broad categories of computer software; operating system software and applications software.

Operating System Software

Operating system software provides the link between the computer hardware, applications software, and the computer user. It consists of programs that start up the computer, retrieve applications programs, and allow the computer operator to store and retrieve data. Operating system software controls access to input and output devices and access to applications programs. There are several popular operating systems for microcomputers. They include Windows 95/98/2000/ME/XP, DOS, DOS combined with Windows 3.XX, OS/2, the Macintosh operating system, and UNIX.

Applications Software

Applications software refers to programs designed for a specific use. The five most common types of business applications software are database management, spreadsheet, word processing, communications, and graphics. Spreadsheet software allows the manipulation of data and has the ability to project answers to "what if" questions. Word processing software enables the user to write and print letters, memos, and other documents. Graphic software display data visually in the form of graphic images, and communications software allows your computer to "talk" to other computers. Most computerized accounting systems are designed as database management software. Accounting information is data that must be organized and stored in a common base of data. This allows the entry of data and the retrieval of information in an organized and systematic way.

Accounting Applications Software   Most computerized accounting software is organized into modules. Each module is designed to process a particular type of accounting data such as accounts receivable, accounts payable, or payroll. Each module is also designed to work in conjunction with the other modules. When modules are designed to work together in this manner, they are referred to as integrated software. In an integrated accounting system each module handles a different function but also communicates with the other modules. For example, to record a sale on account, you would make an entry into the accounts receivable module. The integration feature automatically records this entry in the sales journal, updates the customer's account in the accounts receivable subsidiary ledger, and posts all accounts affected in the general ledger. Thus in an integrated accounting system, transaction data are only entered once. All of the other accounting procedures required to bring the accounting records up-to-date are performed automatically through the integration function.

Peachtree Complete Accounting 2005   The most current version of Peachtree Complete Accounting 2005 has been selected for use in this text to demonstrate and help you learn how to use a computerized accounting system. It is easy to use, fully integrated, and is also available in versions that work with several different operating systems. The program can be used to maintain the accounting data for a sole proprietorship, a partnership or a corporation. It will accommodate service, merchandising and manufacturing businesses. The payroll functions in this version are contrived and should not be used for real payroll calculations. The workshops contained in this text are designed to illustrate how manual accounting concepts will be handled by a computerized accounting system. They are not intended to provide a comprehensive course of study for a computerized accounting system.

WORKING WITH PEACHTREE COMPLETE ACCOUNTING 2005

Before you begin to work with Peachtree Complete Accounting 2005 you need to be familiar with your computer hardware and the Windows operating system. When you are running Windows, your work takes place on the desktop. Think of this area as resembling the surface of a desk. There are physical objects on your real desk and there are windows and icons on the Windows desktop. There are minor differences between the various versions of Windows. The figures will reflect a typical Windows 98 Desktop. Other Windows versions will have small differences but will be essentially the same.

A mouse is an essential input device for all Windows applications. A mouse is a pointing device that assumes different shapes on your monitor as you move the mouse on your desk. According to the nature of the current action, the mouse pointer may appear as a small arrowhead, an hourglass, or a hand. There are five basic mouse techniques:

◆	Click	To quickly press and release the left mouse button.
◆	Double-click	To click the left mouse button twice in rapid succession.
◆	Drag	To hold down the left mouse button while you move the mouse.
◆	Point	To position the mouse pointer over an object without clicking a button.
◆	Right-click	To quickly press and release the right mouse button.

The Windows 98 Desktop

Figure A-4 shows a typical opening Windows 98 screen. Your desktop may be different, just as your real desk is arranged differently from those of your colleagues.

◆ **Desktop icons:** Graphic representations of drives, files, and other resources. The desktop icons that display will vary depending on your computer setup.
◆ **Start button:** Clicking on the Start button displays the start menu and lets you start applications.
◆ **Taskbar:** Contains the start button and other buttons representing open applications.

FIGURE A-
4
Windows
98 Desktop
(Partial)

Applications Window

As you work with Peachtree Complete Accounting 2005 two kinds of windows will appear on your desktop. The Main Menu window is where all activities in Peachtree will begin. An application window contains a running application. The name of the applications and the application's menu bar will appear at the top of the application window. Regardless of the windows that are open on your desktop, most windows have certain elements in common.

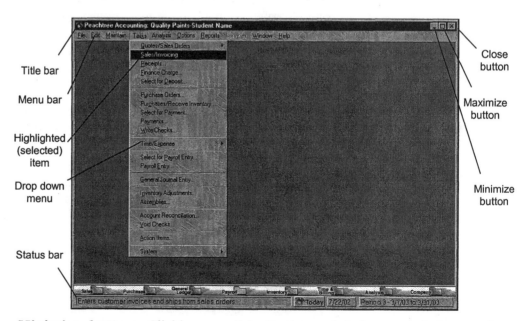

FIGURE A-
5
Peachtree
Main Menu
Application
s Window

- ♦ **Minimize button:** Clicking on this button minimizes a window and displays it as a task button on the taskbar.
- ♦ **Maximize button:** Clicking on this button enlarges the window so that it fills the entire desktop. After you enlarge a window, the maximize button is

replaced by a Restore button (a double box, not shown) that returns the window to the size it was before it was maximized.

♦ **Close button:** Clicking on this button will close the window.

♦ **Title bar:** Displays the name of the application.

♦ **Menu bar:** This window element lists the available menus for the window.

♦ **Drop Down Menu:** Shows the options available under each menu option.

♦ **Highlighted (selected) Item:** The active selection in a Drop Down Menu.

♦ **Status bar:** A line of text at the bottom of many windows that gives more information about a field. If you are unsure of what to enter in a field, select it with your mouse and read the status bar.

Dialog Boxes

A dialog box appears when additional information is needed to execute a command. There are different ways to supply that information; consequently, there are different types of dialog boxes. Most dialog boxes (see Fig. A-6) are for specific functions and tasks and require you to supply the data for that task. After you supply the needed information, you can choose a command button to carry out a command such as to Post or Print.

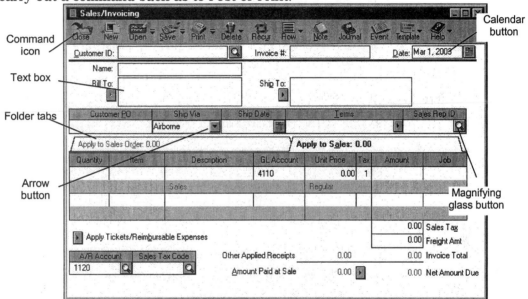

**FIGURE A-6
Peachtree
Sales/Invoicin
g Dialog Box**

♦ **Folder tabs:** Some dialog boxes have multiple pages of entry fields available to them. These tabs allow you to switch between available screens.

♦ **Arrow button:** A button with an arrow will generally bring up a pull down menu of options for that field.

♦ **Text box:** When you move to an empty text box, an insertion point appears in the far left-hand side of the box. The text you type starts at the insertion point. If the box you move to already contains text, this text is selected (highlighted), and any text you type replaces it. You can also delete the selected text by pressing the DELETE or BACKSPACE key.

♦ **Command icons:** Choose (click) on a command icon to initiate an immediate action such as carrying out or canceling a command. The Close, Print and Post buttons are common command buttons.

♦ **Magnifying glass button:** Click on this button to pull down a list of choices. Some fields will not show the magnifying glass until the field has been selected.

♦ **Calendar button:** Click on the this button to bring up a calendar in order to select the date to be inserted in the field next to the button.

Other dialog boxes (see Fig. A-7) may require that choices be made, request additional information, provide warnings, or give messages indicating why a requested task cannot be accomplished.

FIGURE A-7 Peachtree Select a Report Dialog Box

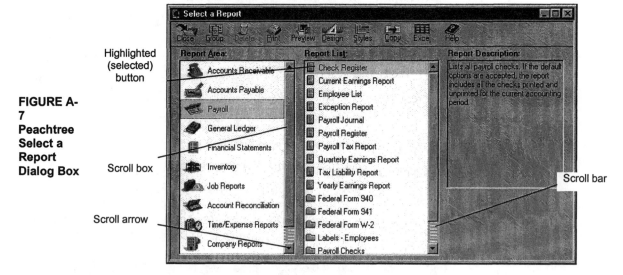

♦ **Highlighted (selected) item:** to highlight and/or select an item in a displayed list, click on the item. Some may require a double click to select. In figure A-7, highlighting an item in the Report Area will bring up a list associated with that item in the Report List box. Highlighting an item in the Report List box will bring up a description in the Report Description box.

♦ **Scroll bar:** A bar that may appear at the bottom and/or right side of a window or dialog box if there is more text than can be displayed at one time within the window.

♦ **Scroll arrow:** A small arrow at the end of a scroll bar that you click on to move to the next item in the list. The top and left arrow scroll to the previous item; the bottom and right arrows scroll to the next item.

♦ **Scroll box:** A small box in a scroll bar. You can use the mouse to drag the scroll box left or right, or up or down. The scroll box indicates the relative position in the list.

Using Menus

Commands are listed on menus, as shown in Figure A-8. Each item on the **Main Menu Bar** has its own menus, which are listed by selecting the menu. When a menu is displayed, choose a command by clicking on it or by typing the **Underlined letter** to execute the command. You can also bypass the menu entirely if you know the **Keyboard equivalent** shown to the right of the command when the menu is displayed.

A **Dimmed command** indicates that a command is not currently executable; some additional action has to be taken for the command to become available. Some commands are followed by **Ellipses** (...) to indicate that more information is required to execute the command. The additional information can be entered into a dialog box, which will appear immediately after the command has been selected.

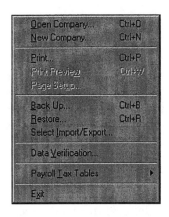

Open Company...	Ctrl+O
New Company...	Ctrl+N
Print...	Ctrl+P
Print Preview	Ctrl+W
Page Setup...	
Back Up...	Ctrl+B
Restore...	Ctrl+R
Select Import/Export...	
Data Verification...	
Payroll Tax Tables	▶
Exit	

Although Peachtree has 10 menu options available on the **Main Menu Bar**, most of your activities will involve the **Maintain**, **Tasks**, or **Reports** menus. The **Tasks** menu contains all of our routine, day to day activities such as invoicing customers, paying vendors, generating payroll, et al. The **Maintain** menu allows us to add, delete and edit customers, vendors, employees and default options, et al. The **Reports** menu allows us to generate the information contained in Peachtree in a variety of formats including custom designed ones.

PART B
Correcting Transactions

Once a transaction is posted in Peachtree Complete Accounting 2005, the journal entry will be reflected in the accounting records. You will however, be allowed to freely edit transactions due to the way the program has been configured for you. Peachtree does have an electronic audit feature that would not allow you to make corrections without creating an audit trail of all such changes. This feature of Peachtree Complete Accounting 2005 is designed to ensure that a good audit trail of all transactions is constantly maintained within the program. This feature is turned on and off in the **Company Information** of the **Maintain** menu option. In a real world working situation, this feature would be turned on. Unless your instructor has you turn this feature on, you will be able to correct errors quickly and easily without creating a record of those corrections.

Correcting Unposted Errors

If you should detect an error while in any of Peachtree's input screens prior to posting or printing, you can quickly and easily correct the error prior to continuing with the transaction.

1. Using your mouse, click in the field that contains the error. This will highlight the selected text box information so that you can change it.

2. Type the correct information; then press the TAB key to enter it. You may then either TAB to other fields needing corrections or again use the mouse to click in the proper field.

3. If you have selected an incorrect account or any other type of look up information, use the pull down menu to select the correct account or information. This will replace the incorrect account with the correct account.

4. To discard an entry and start over, click on the Delete icon. You will not be given the opportunity to verify this step so be sure you want to delete the transaction before selecting this option. This option may not be available on every input screen.

5. Review the entry for accuracy after any editing corrections.

6. Complete the transaction by posting or printing.

Correcting Posted Errors

Should you detect an error after you have posted the transaction, it can still be quickly and easily corrected. The only additional step needed to correct a posted transaction is to find it and bring it up on your screen.

Generate an on-screen report which will contain the document needing correction. As an example, a sales invoice can be found in an Aged Receivables Report, an Invoice Register or a Sales Journal. A General Journal entry can be found in a General Journal or a General Ledger report.

Select the line containing the item needing correction by single clicking the mouse cursor. This will place a blue box around the line and the cursor will turn into a magnifying glass with a Z in the center. Peachtree Complete 2005 comes packaged with a sample company called Bellwether Garden Supply. Looking at a General Journal report under the Reports menu your screen will look like this:

Bellwether Garden Supply
General Journal
For the Period From Mar 1, 2003 to Mar 31, 2003
Filter Criteria includes: Report order is by Date. Report is printed with Accounts having Zero Amounts and in Detail Format.

Date	Account ID	Reference	Trans Description	Debit Amt	Credit Amt
3/10/03	40000-FU	SA031003	Sale of Conference Room table- fully depreciated		15,000.00
	10400		Sale of Conference Room table- fully depreciated	15,000.00	
3/12/03	10300	PYRL031203	Trasnfer From Regular to Payroll Checking	10,000.00	
	10200		Trasnfer From Regular to Payroll Checking		10,000.00
3/31/03	64000	FA032003	Depreciation Expense - 03 2003	2,761.30	
	17000		Depreciation Expense - 03 2003		420.80
	17100		Depreciation Expense - 03 2003		385.05
	17200		Depreciation Expense - 03 2003		1,437.89
	17300		Depreciation Expense - 03 2003		64.57
	17500		Depreciation Expense - 03 2003		396.37
	17600		Depreciation Expense - 03 2003		56.62
3/31/03	17000	ADJ0303103	Miscellaneous reconciling entry	0.04	
	17100		Miscellaneous reconciling entry	0.06	
	17500		Miscellaneous reconciling entry	0.01	
	17600		Miscellaneous reconciling entry		0.01
	89000		Miscellaneous reconciling entry		0.10
		Total		27,761.41	27,761.41

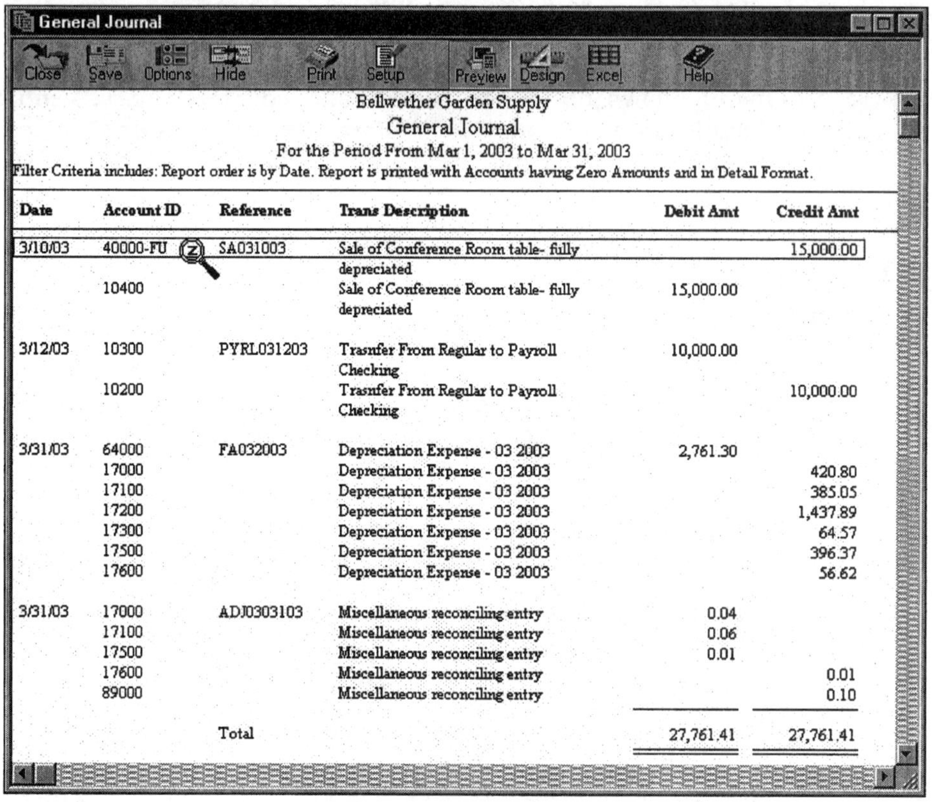

Figure C-1 General Journal

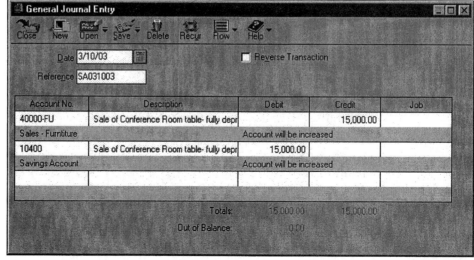

By double clicking on any selected line, you can bring up that particular transaction. If for example, we double click the selection from figure C-1, we are presented with the following:

Figure C-2 General Journal Entry

We could now edit any field of this entry and **Po_st** it again. The procedures that were presented for correcting an unposted transaction can now be applied. You can experiment with this feature in the sample company if your program has Bellwether installed.

PART C
Print and Display Setting in Peachtree Complete

When you install Peachtree Accounting, the program automatically installs the printer established as the default Windows printer as the default printer for Peachtree Accounting. If you have not yet installed a default printer in Windows, you will need to do so prior to attempting to print any reports from the Peachtree Accounting program. Refer to your Windows manual for information on installing a printer.

The installation process for the Windows default printer does not ensure that the default printer and display settings within Peachtree Accounting will work to your satisfaction; consequently, you must test and if necessary adjust your printer and display settings before you complete any of the assignments in the text. Once the print and display settings are adjusted, they will become the default printer and display settings for each set of company data files. You need only make these adjustments once.

If you need to change the font sizes or typefaces on your reports, you can do that from within Peachtree. Each report that you select will have an Options button as illustrated in Figure F-1.

**Figure F-1
Options
Button**

Selecting Options will bring up a dialog box with multiple tabs containing various parameters that can be changed for the report. One of these tabs is Fonts from which you can change the font for each item on the report. See Figure F-2.

**Figure F-2
Fonts Tab**

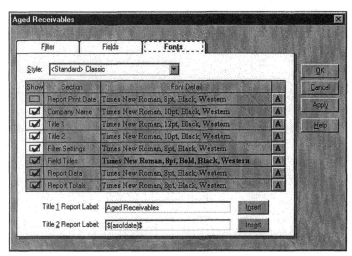